LIGHTHOUSES SERIES

LIGHTHOUSES OF MAINE

A Guidebook and Keepsake

Bruce Roberts and Ray Jones

INSIDERS' GUIDE®

GUILFORD, CONNECTICUT
AN IMPRINT OF THE GLOBE PEQUOT PRESS

INSIDERS' GUIDE®

Copyright © 2006 by Bruce Roberts and Ray Jones

All rights reserved. No part of this book may be reproduced or transmitted in any form by any
means, electronic or mechanical, including photocopying and recording, or by any information
storage and retrieval system, except as may be expressly permitted by the 1976 Copyright Act
or by the publisher. Requests for permission should be made in writing to The Globe Pequot
Press, P.O. Box 480, Guilford, Connecticut 06437.

Insiders' Guide is a registered trademark of Morris Book Publishing, LLC. All Rights Reserved.
Text design by Schwartzman Design, Deep River, CT
Map design and terrain by Stephen C. Stringall, Cartography by M.A. Dubé
Map © Morris Book Publishing, LLC. All Rights Reserved.
All photographs are by Bruce Roberts unless otherwise credited.

Library of Congress Cataloging-in-Publication Data
Roberts, Bruce, 1930–
    Lighthouses of Maine : a guidebook and keepsake / Bruce Roberts and Ray Jones. – 1st ed.
      p. cm – (Lighthouses series)
    ISBN 0-7627-3966-5
      1. Lighthouses–Maine–Guidebooks. I. Jones, Ray, 1948– II. Title. III. Lighthouses series
(Globe Pequot Press)

VK1024.M2R63 2005
387.1'55'09741–dc22

                               2005014166

Manufactured in China
First Edition/First Printing

The information listed in this guide was confirmed at press time. The ownership of many
lighthouses, however, is gradually being transferred from the Coast Guard to private
concerns. Please confirm visitor information before traveling.

CONTENTS

INTRODUCTION 1

CHAPTER ONE: WAY DOWNEAST: FROM
WHITLOCKS MILL TO ACADIA NATIONAL PARK 8

Whitlocks Mill Light 10
Lubec Channel Light 11
West Quoddy Head Light 12
Little River Light 14
Petit Manan Light 15
Prospect Harbor Point Light 16
Winter Harbor Lighthouse 18
Egg Rock Light 20
Bear Island Light 22
Blue Hill Bay Light 23
Bass Harbor Head Light 24
Baker Island Light 26
Great Duck Island Light 27
Mount Desert Rock Light 28
Burnt Coat Harbor Light 30
Isle au Haut Light 32

CHAPTER TWO: THE MIDDLE COAST: FROM PENOBSCOT BAY
TO BOOTHBAY HARBOR 34

Saddleback Ledge Light 36
Deer Island Thoroughfare Light 37
Eagle Island Light 38
Dice Head Light 40
Fort Point Light 42
Goose Rocks Light 43
Grindle Point Light 44
Curtis Island Light 45
Rockland Breakwater Light 46
Owls Head Light 48
Browns Head Light 50
Heron Neck Light 52
Two Bush Island Light 54
Matinicus Rock Light 56
Whitehead Light 58
Tenants Harbor Lighthouse 59

Marshall Point Light 60
Pemaquid Point Light 62
Ram Island Light..64
Hendricks Head Light 66
Cuckolds Light 68
Monhegan Island Light 69

CHAPTER THREE: DOWN PORTLAND WAY:
FROM BATH TO KITTERY 70
Seguin Island Light 72
Doubling Point Range Lights 74
Halfway Rock Light 76
Ram Island Ledge Light 77
Portland Breakwater Light 78
Spring Point Ledge Light 80
Portland Head Light..82
Cape Elizabeth Light 84
Wood Island Light 86
Boon Island Light 87
Cape Neddick Light 88
Whaleback Ledge Light 90

GLOSSARY 91

DEDICATION

To Cheryl Shelton-Roberts, my wife and the light of my life
—Bruce Roberts

For Tim and Kathy
—Ray Jones

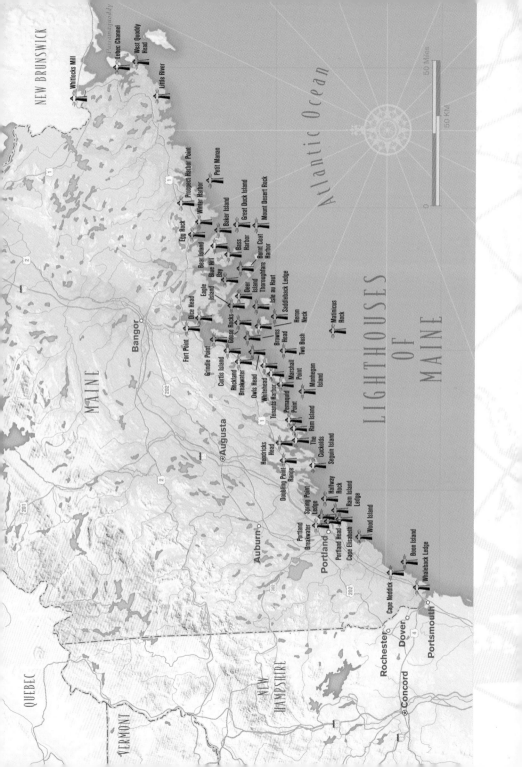

INTRODUCTION

In the language of sailors, Maine is "downeast," meaning that it trends toward the Atlantic. Seamen are cautious when they go downeast, for these are not charitable shores, and the land and sea come together here in dramatic and often violent ways. For this reason and others, Maine is a place of many lighthouses.

Clawed by glaciers during the great ice ages, the coast of Maine is a labyrinth of points and passages, of fjord-like fingers of salt water reaching 50 miles or more inland, and of rocky peninsulas extended like talons into the sea. Nearly 3,500 miles of shoreline are crammed inlet upon inlet into the state's 228 miles of coast. When confronting this maze, out-of-state motorists need a good map, a full tank of gas, and plenty of patience. When sailing into it, mariners need the best charts available, an intuitive sense of tides and currents, and a beacon.

For more than two centuries, lighthouses have served as signposts marking the turns and terrors of the Maine coast, warning sailors and fishermen away from knife-edged rocks and guiding them safely to port. To the delight of tourists and native Mainers alike, many of these historic and picturesque sentinels still stand and still serve mariners. These guardians of light are the subject of this book.

Shepherds of Waves

Unfortunately, the profession of lighthouse keeping is now all but extinct. Driven by budget cuts and demands for ever-greater efficiency, the U.S. Coast Guard has automated one lighthouse after another. Technology has replaced the sharp eyes and strong, steady fingers of keepers with automatic timers, radio relays, and satellite transmissions. Although they continue the necessary work of marking dangerous obstacles and guiding vessels safely to port, the downeast lighthouses now stand their vigils alone. In earlier times, however—in fact, until about the middle of the twentieth century—that was not the case. The lights could do their jobs only with the help of lonely, hard-working lighthouse keepers.

Isolation breeds eloquence. For proof of this, one need only turn to the logs and letters of downeast lighthouse keepers. As members of a profession that paid them barely enough to live, these rugged, rawboned men and women were frugal in all things, even in their use of language. Nature and circumstance taught them to place a special value on words.

Some have counted lighthouse keepers among the world's best storytellers. Wordsmiths the likes of Henry Wadsworth Longfellow and Henry David Thoreau have smoked pipes and sipped mugs of coffee with Maine keepers and felt tingles running up their spines at stories of storm, shipwreck, sacrifice, and heroism. Thoreau especially admired the keeper's way of spinning a tale, not with miles of silk but with a few yards of good, stout yarn. In the following and later passages in *Lighthouses of Maine,* keepers tell what it was like to live in a lighthouse.

The Worst Sea Is Coming

Keepers usually lived at lighthouses with their families, who faced the loneliness, hardship, danger, and punishing weather along with them. Family members often shared the heavy work of keeping the lights burning, frequently displaying the same heroic resolve as the keepers themselves. The following tale illustrates the hardiness and dedication of lighthouse families.

During the holiday season, Cape Neddick Light serves as an offshore Christmas tree.
Ross Tracy

On a stormy night in 1856, young Abbie Burgess drew up a chair to the kitchen table at the battered keeper's residence on

Matinicus Rock, Maine, and dipped her pen into ink. A lonely seventeen-year-old, separated by at least 25 miles of turbulent sea from the nearest barn dance, church social, or country store, she had decided to write a letter to a pen pal on the mainland:

You have often expressed a desire to view the sea out on the ocean when it was angry. Had you been here on 19 January [1856], I surmise you would have been satisfied. Father was away. Early in the day, as the tide rose, the sea made a complete breach over the rock, washing every movable thing away, and of the old dwelling not one stone was left upon another. The new dwelling was flooded, and the windows had to be secured to prevent the violence of the spray from breaking them in. As the tide came, the sea rose higher and higher, till the only endurable places were the light towers. If they stood, we were saved, otherwise our fate was only too certain. But for some reason, I know not why, I had no misgivings, and went on with my work as usual. For four weeks, owing to rough weather, no landing could be effected on the rock. During this time we were without assistance of any male member of our family. Though at times greatly exhausted with my labors, not once did the lights fail. I was able to perform all my accustomed duties as well as my father's.

   You know the hens are our only companions. Becoming convinced, as the gale increased, that unless they were brought into the house they would be lost, I said to my mother, "I must try to save them." She advised me not to attempt it. The thought, however, of parting with them without an effort was not to be endured, so seizing a basket, I ran out a few yards after the rollers had passed and the sea fell off a little, with the water knee deep, to the coop, and rescued all but one. It was the work of a moment, and I was back in the house with the door fastened, but I was none too quick, for at that instant my little sister, standing at the window, exclaimed, "Oh look! look there! The worst sea is coming." That wave destroyed the old dwelling and swept the rock. I cannot think you would enjoy remaining here any great length of time for the sea is never still and when agitated, its roar shuts out every other sound, even drowning our voices.

A few years after the extraordinary month-long Atlantic storm described in her letter, Abbie Burgess married a lighthouse keeper. She and her husband eventually became assistant keepers of the Matinicus Rock Light.

The Frozen Lovers

Every word of Abbie Burgess' story is true. Then, of course, there are those other sorts of stories spun up on a cold, dark night by keepers not inclined to, as they say, "put too fine a point on the truth." One such yarn—and we'll stand behind every word of it—is the following story of the Frozen Lovers.

A few days before Christmas in the year 1850, a small coasting schooner dropped anchor off Jameson's Point. The vessel was without its captain, who had gone ashore in nearby Rockland and mysteriously disappeared. Some say the captain had been fired; others say he had a premonition and decided to flee from fate. But the schooner's mate, who knew nothing of any dark premonition, saw his master's absence as an opportunity. He had recently proposed to a lovely young woman, and with no one to order him otherwise, he invited her to his cabin.

Only the mate, his bride-to-be, and a deckhand were aboard on the evening of December 22, when a vicious winter gale blew in off the ocean and snapped the schooner's cables. Although the sailors fought hard to save their vessel, the storm drove it relentlessly forward, finally crushing its hull on the cruel ledges near Owls Head. Held in a viselike grip by the rocks, the schooner filled with seawater but did not sink. Instead, it became a target for giant waves, which threw spouts of freezing spray over the three frightened people huddled on its deck. Their clothes and even their skin quickly became rough and crusty with ice.

The mate knew that he and his fellow shipwreck victims would soon freeze to death unless something was done. Faced with the horror of having coaxed his beloved into an apparent death trap, he came up with a desperate plan. To save themselves, he and his companions would roll up in a blanket and lie down together beside the stern rail. The mate hoped the freezing spray would form a protective shell of ice on the outside of the blanket. This it did, but the ice grew much thicker than he had anticipated. All night the sea continued to douse the three until they were entombed in a layer of ice several inches thick.

Under the suffocating weight of the ice, the mate and his girl lost consciousness, and by morning the deckhand believed that he was the only one left alive. Slashing at the ice with a small knife and using his bleeding hands as hammers, he managed to free himself. When he was strong enough to stand, the sailor saw that the tide had gone out and a narrow bridge of exposed rock now connected the schooner with the shore. So, bloodied and nearly frozen, he dropped down off the deck and stumbled off toward the Owls Head Light, which he could see shining through the storm. Overwhelmed by cold and exhaustion, he made the last part of the journey crawling on his hands and knees. But he eventually reached his destination, and in the warm kitchen of the keeper's dwelling, he told his incredible story.

The keeper had little hope of finding anyone alive aboard the schooner; nevertheless, he organized a rescue party and headed for the wreck. There the rescuers found a man and a woman locked in a lover's embrace and frozen in a solid block of ice. It took picks, chisels, knives, and several strong men to free the pair. Everyone was sure they were dead; even so, an attempt was made to revive them. Hurried ashore to a home near the lighthouse, their seemingly lifeless bodies were treated with cold-water baths and constant massage. In two hours the woman regained consciousness. An hour after that the mate also showed signs of life. It took the two several months to recover from their ordeal, but by June they were strong enough to stand together in front of a preacher and pronounce their vows.

Ironically, the sailor whose grueling trek through the storm had brought help and saved the lovers from certain death never fully recovered from his adventure. He did not go to sea again and lived out his life on waterfronts of towns near Owls Head. He never tired of telling strangers about his struggle in the blizzard of 1850 and about the frozen lovers of Owls Head.

How to Use This Guide

Your own Maine lighthouse adventure need not be quite so thrilling or dangerous. Even so you can get a strong sense of what it was like living hard against the sea when you read about the beautiful and historic light towers featured in *Lighthouses of Maine*—even more so—when you visit them yourself.

Maine can boast more than sixty standing lighthouses, more than any other state except Michigan, and every one is worth a visit. This book takes you to every Maine lighthouse that can be reached and to some that are inaccessible. As you'll see, the book is divided into three sections: Way Downeast: from Whitlocks Mill to Acadia National Park, The Middle Coast: from Penobscot Bay to Boothbay Harbor, and Down Portland Way: from Bath to Kittery. Within the sections lighthouses are presented in geographic order, just as they might appear on the map. This arrangement should make it easier to plan your own Maine lighthouse outings—so should the directions, telephone contacts, and other travel information included at the end of each listing.

Under normal circumstances, you should be able to visit the most attractive lighthouses in one or another of the sections mentioned above in a single long weekend excursion from Portland, Bangor, or Bar Harbor. To help you select the lighthouses you want to visit, individual listings include advice in the form simple symbols: 🏛 for lighthouses that are especially historic—most of them are, 🚪 for lighthouses that are accessible—more than a few are not, 🏞 for visitor-friendly lighthouses that are frequently open to the public and feature museums or similar attractions, and 📷 for lighthouses that make great pictures—most of them are quite photogenic. A fifth symbol ⚓ indicates those lost lighthouses, historic towers that, unfortunately, no longer exist. For added convenience, each listing also includes an easy-to-read summary of key information on the lighthouse: location, date the light was established, height of the tower, elevation of the beacon, type of optic, current status, characteristic, range, and for all active lighthouses, the precise longitude and latitude of the station.

We hope you enjoy your Maine lighthouse adventure.

Clawed by ancient
glaciers, the rocks at
Pemaquid Point resemble
waves.

CHAPTER ONE
WAY DOWNEAST: FROM WHITLOCKS MILL TO ACADIA NATIONAL PARK

In the minds of many native Mainers, the true downeast does not include the entire state. Rather it begins with the highlands of Mount Desert and Acadia National Park and extends eastward toward Calais, the St. Croix River, and the Canadian border. The rugged shores of this region are dotted with quaint, clapboard villages the likes of Eastport, Lubec, Cutler, Jonesport, and Winter Harbor. Time stands still for these very old but still vibrant maritime communities where little changes except the weather. Even in summer the downeast weather can be quite bracing, if not altogether terrible.

To help fishermen and other mariners find their way safely to harbor despite fog, blizzards, or sea storms, a scatter of lighthouses mark the entrances to prominent coves and inlets or stand guard over wave-swept rocks, ledges, and other dangerous obstacles. Located on remote promontories or barren islands, these sentinels rank among the world's most isolated navigational stations, and the men and women who once served as their keepers surely numbered among our nation's loneliest public servants. Consequently, they nearly always welcomed visitors, even half-drowned seamen.

Wreck on Mount Desert Rock

Since they lived on the most dangerous stretches of coast, keepers often witnessed calamitous wrecks and nearly as often helped drag survivors out of the surf. For shipwrecked sailors, a keeper might serve as rescuer, physician, and innkeeper.

A keeper on Mount Desert Rock, Maine, left the following record of the early twentieth-century wreck of the tug *Astral*:

It was on December 9th, 1902 at 5 o'clock in the morning that the second assistant keeper whose morning watch it was, called me saying "I think I heard a steamboat blow a blast of seven whistles as if in distress."

I jumped out of bed and dressed as quickly as possible. The vapor was flying so high and densely that one could see hardly ten feet ahead. It was inky dark and blowing one of the worst gales I had seen since being in the service.

The thermometer never had dropped so low during the thirteen years I had been on the Rock. The assistant had noticed that the sounds of the whistle came from the northeast and so we went in that direction. It was then high tide but we could, after a fashion, make out that there was some kind of steamer ashore on the northeast point; but as the big seas were running so mountain high it would have meant suicide for any of us to try to get out where she was.

The seas were running through between the main rock and the outer point. I could see that no boat could live to get to the outer point and across the expanse of rough water. We called and called, trying to get an answer. Not hearing or seeing anything, we stayed where we were until we nearly froze to death. We could not stand the terrific cold air and simply had to get back to the station. We were chilled to the bones and could hardly speak when we got into the house.

My wife had plenty of boiling water and a big pot of coffee ready to serve instantly. As soon was we got thawed out so we could handle our fingers we began getting down ropes and life preservers as near the wreck as we could. We were compelled to wait until the tide went down and then we got across to the outer point. We could then see that it was a large ocean tug with a barge in tow. The terrific blows that the sea was pounding on the craft would turn her almost completely over. Between the seas I was able to get a line to them and, one by one, we succeeded in rescuing seventeen men.

There were eighteen in the crew but one was frozen to death before we could get him ashore. They were all more or less frozen, and badly at that. The second engineer of the tug had to be carried to the house, his limbs being useless. He was in terrible condition. Well, after we got them all to the house we treated their frostbites and got them a hot breakfast. That night we doused them with quinine pills and hot lemonade for fear they might come down with bad colds and pneumonia might set in.

WHITLOCKS MILL LIGHT

Location: Near Calais

Established: 1909

Tower height: 25 feet

Elevation of the focal plane: 32 feet

Optic: Modern

Status: Active

Characteristic: Green light blinks every 6 seconds

Range: 5 miles

Position: 45° 09' 48
67° 13' 36

Note: A river light located near the Canadian border

One of several small U.S. and Canadian beacons that formerly guided lumber freighters along the St. Croix River to the port of Calais, the Whitlocks Mill Light dates from 1909. Its 25-foot masonry tower replaced an early stone lighthouse that had stood here since 1892. An automated optic replaced the fourth-order Fresnel lens in 1969. The light remains active, flashing green ten times a minute. The St. Croix Lighthouse, which at one time stood a few miles downriver from this one, was destroyed by fire in 1976.

TO SEE THE LIGHT: Travelers can see the tower from the St. Croix View Rest Area on U.S. Highway 1 a few miles east of Calais and about 5 miles northwest of the St. Croix Island International Historic Site. Contact the St. Croix Historical Society, P.O. Box 242, Calais, ME 04619.

Bob and Sandra Shanklin, The Lighthouse People

Most vessels approaching the St. Croix River ports of Lubec, Eastport, and Calais use the narrow Lubec Channel, which separates Maine from Canada's Campobello Island to the north of Quoddy Head. To make this key passage safer, the U.S. government marked it with an open-water light station in 1890. Built on a massive caisson of concrete and iron, the station's brick-lined, cast-iron tower rises 53 feet above the water. When seen from a distance, light-houses of this type resemble giant spark plugs.

In the past hardy keepers and their assistants lived year-round in cramped quarters on the lower level. The station was automated after a destructive oil fire in 1939. Prior to that time and for nearly eighty years, the beacon was produced by a fifth-order, bull's-eye Fresnel lens rotated by a weight-driven clockwork mechanism. A plastic optic replaced the original lens in 1969. Now solar powered, the light remains active, flashing green ten times a minute.

Bob and Sandra Shanklin,

The Lighthouse People

TO SEE THE LIGHT: Although closed to the public, the light can be seen from South Lubec Road, off Route 189 on the way to Quoddy Head State Park. The best views can be had from the roadside about one-half mile south of Lubec.

Location: Lubec

Established: 1890

Tower height: 53 feet

Elevation of the focal plane: 53 feet

Optic: Modern (solar powered)

Status: Active

Characteristic: Flashes every 6 seconds

Range: 6 miles

Position: 44° 50' 30
66° 38' 36

Note: A "sparkplug" tower built in open water atop a massive caisson

WEST QUODDY HEAD LIGHT

ooking out across the Quoddy Narrows from its perch on a 40-foot cliff, West Quoddy Head Light anchors the easternmost point in the United States (East Quoddy Head Light, across the narrows, is on Canada's Campobello Island). Established in 1808, while Thomas Jefferson was still president, this is one of Maine's oldest light stations. The original rubble-stone tower was torn down and rebuilt with brick in 1858. At that time the station received the third-order Fresnel lens that still guides ships and fishing vessels into Lubec Channel. The light atop the 49-foot, candy-striped tower flashes white four times each minute and can be seen from a distance of up to 18 nautical miles.

Equipped with a strobe light and an electric eye that senses moisture in the air, the station's powerful foghorn occupies a separate brick building. Earlier fog signals here included a black-powder cannon, a 1,500-pound bell, and a steam whistle.

TO SEE THE LIGHT: From U.S. Highway 1 turn toward Lubec on Route 189; then turn right at the sign for Quoddy Head State Park. The park charges a small entrance fee but offers world-class views of Grand Manan Channel, nature trails featuring real tundra, and a chance to walk the lighthouse grounds at leisure. Contact West Quoddy Head Light Keepers Association, P.O. Box 378, Lubec, ME 04652; (207) 733–2180.

Location: Lubec

Established: 1808

Tower height: 49 feet

Elevation of the focal
plane: 83 feet

Optic: Fresnel
(third order)

Status: Active

Characteristic: Flashes
twice every 15 seconds

Range: 18 miles

Position: 44° 48' 54
66° 57' 00

Note: Most easterly light
in the United States

LITTLE RIVER LIGHT

Established during the mid-nineteenth century, the Little River Light station served mariners for nearly 130 years before being shut down by the Coast Guard in 1975. The 41-foot iron tower and L-shaped Victorian dwelling stood empty and neglected for many years. The U.S. Coast Guard put the old light station up for sale during the 1990s, but at first there were no takers. Finally, the deteriorating light came under the wing of the American Lighthouse Foundation, which acquired the property in 2000. Although the badly weathered structures are still considered endangered, they are being restored, and the tower was relit in 2001.

TO SEE THE LIGHT: Located on an island near Cutler off Route 191 in far eastern Maine, the light cannot be seen from the mainland and isn't open to the public. However, local wildlife and sightseeing cruises offer excellent views of the Little River Light as well as the Machias Seal Islands Light Station (1832) southeast of Cutler and the Libby Island Light Station near Machias; call (207) 259–4484. For more information on the American Lighthouse Foundation and its wide-ranging preservation efforts, contact P.O. Box 889, Wells, ME 04090; (207) 646–0245.

Location: Cutler

Established: 1847

Tower height: 41 feet

Elevation of the focal plane: 57 feet

Optic: Modern

Status: Active

Characteristic: Flashes every 6 seconds

Range: 13 miles

Position: 44° 39' 03
67° 11' 32

Note: Being restored by the American Lighthouse Foundation

American Lighthouse Foundation

Bob and Sandra Shanklin,
The Lighthouse People

During the early nineteenth century, coasting schooners were often forced to heel hard to port to avoid the deadly rocks of Petit Manan Island. A lighthouse built there in 1817 did little to improve the situation. Shining from atop a rubble-stone tower only 53-feet tall, its old-fashioned Winslow Lewis lamps were so limited in range that sailors could barely see the beacon until they were almost upon the rocks. For more than a few mariners, the warning came too late.

In 1855 the Lighthouse Board sought to prevent further shipping losses by ordering construction of a soaring 119-foot brick-and-granite tower on Petit Manan. Focused by a powerful second-order Fresnel lens, its flashing light pulsed a warning more than 25 miles out to sea. The Fresnel was replaced in 1972 by an automated optic of similar range. The light flashes six times each minute.

TO SEE THE LIGHT: From U.S. Highway 1 near Milbridge, turn south on Pigeon Hill Road and follow it to the Petit Manan Wildlife Refuge. A scenic 2-mile-long trail leads to the east side of Petit Manan Point, where visitors can enjoy an excellent view of the light.

Location:	Near Milbridge
Established:	1817
Tower height:	119 feet
Elevation of the focal plane:	123 feet
Optic:	Modern
Status:	Active
Characteristic:	Flashes every 10 seconds
Range:	19 miles
Position:	44° 22' 0 67° 51' 5
Note:	Site of a rare breeding colony of puffins

PROSPECT HARBOR POINT LIGHT

Prospect Harbor Point Light looks much like a fisherman's cottage—except for the 38-foot conical tower rising from its seaward wall. Its design is appropriate since its beacon shines out mostly to lobster and sardine boats. Built in 1891, the two-story, wood-frame structure replaced an earlier granite lighthouse that first marked the point in 1850. Ironically, the stone light tower succumbed to the elements after little more than forty years, yet its wooden replacement perseveres, despite weathering over a century of storms. Nowadays, the dwelling serves as a guesthouse for visitors to the adjacent naval base. The light remains active, flashing red and white ten times a minute.

TO SEE THE LIGHT: From U.S. Highway 1, follow either Route 186 or Route 195 to Prospect Harbor. Although open to the general public on Memorial Day weekend and during the Winter Harbor Lobster Festival, the light can be seen and photographed from several viewpoints in the village. The handsomely maintained dwelling occasionally serves as a vacation rental for military retirees. For information, contact Navy Satellite Operations Center, P.O. Box 229, Attention: Detachment Alpha, Officer-in-Charge, Prospect Harbor, ME 04669; (207) 963–7700.

Location: Prospect Harbor

Established: 1850

Tower height: 38 feet

Elevation of the focal plane: 42 feet

Optic: Modern

Status: Active

Characteristic: Flashes red every 6 seconds (two white sectors)

Range: 7 miles

Position: 44° 24' 12 68° 00' 48

Note: Used as a guesthouse by the military

Ronald J. Foster

WINTER HARBOR LIGHTHOUSE

Motorists on the perimeter road of Acadia National Park's Schoodic Point often notice a small white-brick light tower and attached Victorian keeper's dwelling. Located on Mark Island, just to the west of Schoodic Peninsula, this is the Winter Harbor Lighthouse, which served from 1856 until 1934, when it was decommissioned. At present the lighthouse is privately owned and maintained.

Many have dreamed of living in a lighthouse or writing a book. Bernice Richmond did both, living at the Winter Habor Lighouse, and later describing her experience in *Our Island Lighthouse*.

TO SEE THE LIGHT: From U.S. Highway 1, follow Route 186 through Winter Harbor to the Acadia National Park entrance; passes are required during the summer season. Parking areas about a mile south of the entrance afford excellent views of the lighthouse. Be sure to stop at Schoodic Point at the far end of the drive. On most days waves crash into the bare rocks of the point and spew high into the air. Don't feed the seagulls, or you'll have hundreds of them hounding you for handouts.

Location: Winter Harbor

Established: 1856

Tower height: 19 feet

Elevation of the focal plane: 37 feet

Status: Deactivated 1934

Note: Author Bernice Richmond wrote *Our Island Lighthouse* here

EGG ROCK LIGHT

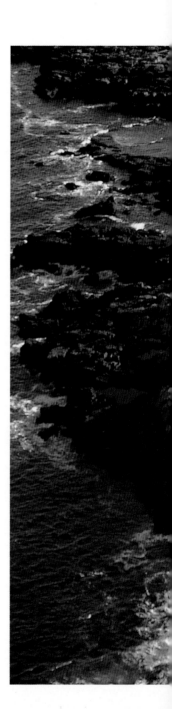

Location: Near Bar Harbor

Established: 1875

Tower height: 40 feet

Elevation of the focal
plane: 64 feet

Optic: Modern

Status: Active

Characteristic: Flashes
red every 5 seconds

Range: 18 miles

Position: 44° 21' 12
68° 08' 18

Note: Can be seen from
Acadia National Park

The dramatic red flash of Egg Rock Light in Frenchman Bay often catches the attention of visitors to Acadia National Park. Once described as a "pillar of fire in the Atlantic," the beacon emanates from a barren ledge, which likely got its name from the countless seabird nests found there during mating season. The signal marks seaward approaches to Bar Harbor. Flashing red at five-second intervals, it can be seen from 18 miles away.

The station's squat, 40-foot tower is far less awe-inspiring than its light. Built in 1875, the squared-off wooden dwelling and brick tower are more functional than scenic. An aeromarine beacon superseded the original fourth-order Fresnel lens when the light was automated in 1976.

TO SEE THE LIGHT: The light can be seen from several scenic overlooks along the Acadia National Park Loop Road on Mount Desert Island. Thundering surf, panoramic ocean views, and the East's loftiest headland—1,500-foot Cadillac Mountain—make this park one of America's must-see scenic wonders. The best time to avoid the summer throngs is before July 4 or after Labor Day. When you go, don't leave without sampling the boiled lobster in Bar Harbor or the popovers and tea at the Jordan Pond House.

BEAR ISLAND LIGHT

Location: South of Mount Desert Island

Established: 1839

Tower height: 33 feet

Elevation of the focal plane: 100 feet

Optic: Modern

Status: Private aid to navigation

Characteristic: Flashes every 5 seconds

Range: Approximately 10 miles

Position: 44° 16' 52
68° 16' 10

Note: Restored and relighted in 1989 by local lighthouse lovers

Bob and Sandra Shanklin,
The Lighthouse People

The Bear Island Light tower is only 33 feet tall, but it stands on the highest point of a rocky islet, elevating the focal plane of its signal to about 100 feet above the water. From its lofty perch, the little light guides fishing boats and pleasure craft into beautiful Northeast Harbor and ferries out to Acadia's timeless Cranberry Islands.

Two earlier lighthouses preceded the present tower and separate dwelling. The first was a rustic stone dwelling and tower built in 1839. The second, completed in 1853, had a separate brick tower that was apparently removed to make way for construction of the existing station in 1889. The Coast Guard deactivated this station in 1981, but local preservationists restored the property and relit the beacon a few years later. A plastic optic now serves in place of the original fifth-order Fresnel lens.

TO SEE THE LIGHT: From the Northeast Harbor Marina, you can see the Bear Island Light in the distance. To reach Northeast Harbor, one of several extraordinarily scenic villages on Mount Desert Island, follow Route 3 and then Route 189 from Ellsworth. The deck of the Cranberry Island ferry offers a closer view of the light. For information on scheduled service from Northeast Harbor during summer, call (207) 276–5352. Acadia National Park offers summer tours of nearby Baker Island, and an excellent view of the Bear Island Light can be had from the park ferry; call (207) 288–3338.

Bob and Sandra Shanklin, The Lighthouse People

ince before the Civil War, the Blue Hill Bay Light has survived wind, weather, and the encroaching sea on tiny Green Island near the entrance to Eggemoggin Reach. Completed in 1857, it served for almost eighty years before its work was taken over by a more easily maintained light mounted on a nearby steel-skeleton tower. In operation since 1935, the automated light in the steel tower guides fishing boats and recreational boaters through the bay. Now privately owned, the old brick tower and attached cape-style dwelling remain standing.

TO SEE THE LIGHT: One of the hardest light stations in Maine to visit or photograph, the Blue Hill Bay Light is difficult to approach from the water and is probably best seen from the air. Aerial sightseeing tours that include flights over this and other lights are available at the Hancock County/Bar Harbor Airport, off Route 3; call (207) 667–6527.

Location: Green Island

Established: 1857

Tower height: 22 feet

Elevation of the focal plane: 26 feet (new steel tower)

Optic: Modern

Status: Active (new steel tower)

Characteristic: Flashes green every 4 seconds

Range: 5 miles

Position: 44° 14' 54
68° 29' 54

Note: Marks the entrance to scenic Eggemoggin Reach

BASS HARBOR HEAD LIGHT

Location: Bass Harbor

Established: 1858

Tower height: 32 feet

Elevation of the focal plane: 56 feet

Optic: Fresnel (fourth order)

Status: Active

Characteristic: Red occulting every 4 seconds

Range: 13 miles

Position: 44° 13' 19 68° 20' 14

Note: Excellent subject for photographs

Thought by many people to be the most picturesque light in America, this compact brick tower and attached wooden dwelling cling to a red-rock cliff near the entrance to Bass Harbor. Located on the western "quiet side" of Mount Desert Island, well away from the tourist throngs of Bar Harbor and Acadia Park Island, Bass Harbor bobs with dozens of brightly painted lobster boats. The station's red light has guided the fishermen of this bucolic village since before the Civil War.

The original fourth-order Fresnel lens remains in place. Its light's focal plane lies about 56 feet above the water. The beam occults, or goes dark briefly, every four seconds. Panels outside the lens create the light's red color.

TO SEE THE LIGHT: Now used as a residence for Coast Guard personnel, the light is not open to the public, but visitors can enjoy it nonetheless. A small park surrounds the station property, and a paved walkway runs right up to the tower. On the far side of the station, a path connects the parking lot with a wooden stairway that leads down the side of the cliff to the reddish boulders below. The short but strenuous climb rewards the adventurous with extraordinary views of the channel and islands beyond and an unmatched opportunity to photograph one of the nation's prettiest lights.

BAKER ISLAND LIGHT

Bob and Sandra Shanklin,
The Lighthouse People

Location: South of Mount
Desert Island

Established: 1828

Tower height: 43 feet

Elevation of the focal
plane: 105 feet

Optic: Modern
(solar powered)

Status: Active

Characteristic: Flashes
every 10 seconds

Range: 10 miles

Position: 44° 13' 30
68° 11' 54

Note: Marks the approach
to Mount Desert Island

Vessels plying the rock-strewn waters near Maine's legendary Mount Desert Island have long relied on the Baker Island Light. Since 1828 it has warned them away from the deadly shoals just off Little Cranberry Island and guided them safely into broad Frenchman's Bay. The original wood-frame lighthouse was replaced in 1855 by the present 43-foot brick tower and separate dwelling.

When William Gilley, the station's first keeper, was dismissed after more than two decades of service, he took the government to court, claiming he owned the island and the lighthouse. Legal squabbling between the U.S. Lighthouse Service and the Gilley family went on for more than forty years before the government finally proved its clear title to the property. Baker Island now belongs to Acadia National Park. The fourth-order Fresnel lens that at one time served here has been replaced by an automated plastic lens powered by batteries. These, in turn, are recharged by solar panels.

TO SEE THE LIGHT: Currently, the light is not open to the public. Contact Acadia National Park, P.O. Box 177, Bar Harbor, ME 04609; call (207) 288–3338.

GREAT DUCK ISLAND LIGHT

Great Duck Island lies under siege by the Atlantic about 5 miles to the south of Bass Harbor. In part because of its remoteness, countless seabirds, including rare petrels and eider ducks, call the island home. For nearly a century the island was also home to a tiny colony of lighthouse keepers and their families, who received weekly deliveries of mail and supplies from the mainland.

Established in 1890, the light is now automated. In 1986 a plastic lens replaced the fifth-order Fresnel lens that formerly crowned its 42-foot granite-and-brick tower. Its red flashing light can be seen for nearly 20 miles.

TO SEE THE LIGHT: At present, the island and most of the station are owned by The Nature Conservancy, which maintains a bird sanctuary here. The island is off limits to the public during the summer nesting season, but occasional bird-watching tours are conducted by Maine chapters of The Nature Conservancy (207–729–5181) or Audubon Society (207–781–2330).

Location: South of Mount Desert Island

Established: 1890

Tower height: 42 feet

Elevation of the focal plane: 67 feet

Optic: Modern (solar powered)

Status: Active

Characteristic: Flashes red every 5 seconds

Range: 19 miles

Position: 44° 08' 30
68° 14' 42

Note: Research center for the College of the Atlantic

MOUNT DESERT ROCK LIGHT

Relentlessly pounded by Atlantic waves, Mount Desert Rock surely ranks as one of the least hospitable places in America. Yet, for nearly 150 years, lighthouse keepers and their families lived on this open ocean ledge, which is only 600 yards long and less than 20 feet above the water at its highest point. So barren was their home that friendly lobster fishermen brought them baskets

U.S. Coast Guard

of soil in the spring so that they could make a little garden in some rain-moistened crevasses among boulders.

Established in 1830 to warn ships away from this exceptionally dangerous obstacle more than 20 miles from the nearest land, the light at first consisted of only a two-story wooden cottage with a lantern on its roof. The light, provided by inefficient Winslow Lewis reflectors, often could not be seen in time to prevent wrecks.

In 1857 the Lighthouse Board had a stone tower built here, equipped with a third-order Fresnel lens. With a focal plane 75 feet above the water, the light was visible more than 20 miles away. Its range was sharply reduced in heavy weather, however. During a winter storm in 1902, the crew of the ocean tug *Astral* did not see the light at all, and their vessel slammed into rock. The keeper and his wife managed to save all but one of those onboard.

Keepers served at this isolated station until 1977, when the light was automated. At that time the old Fresnel lens was replaced by a plastic lens. The light flashes white four times each minute.

TO SEE THE LIGHT: Mount Desert Rock is, of course, very hard to reach, but whale-watching cruises operating out of Bar Harbor often take passengers within sight of the ledge and its light. For information contact the Bar Harbor Chamber of Commerce, P.O. Box 158, Bar Harbor, ME 04609; (207) 288–3393.

Location: South of Mount Desert Island

Established: 1830

Tower height: 58 feet

Elevation of the focal plane: 75 feet

Optic: Modern (solar powered)

Status: Active

Characteristic: Flashes every 15 seconds

Range: 20 miles

Position: 43° 58' 06
68° 07' 42

Note: Whale-watching station for the College of the Atlantic

BURNT COAT HARBOR LIGHT

Burnt Coat Harbor may have gotten its name from a Revolutionary deserter. Seeking refuge from the storm of war then breaking over the country, a soldier named Thomas Kench symbolically "burned his coat" and fled to the island in 1776. Vessels seeking refuge here from more natural storms have all too often ended up on the island's deadly rocks. To make the harbor—the primary anchorage for lobstermen on Maine's sleepy Swans Island—easier and safer to reach, a lighthouse was built on Hockamock Head near its entrance in 1872.

At first a pair of range lights marked the safe channel, but these so confused local sailors that wrecks occurred even faster than before. To simplify matters, the Lighthouse Board ordered the smaller of the two towers pulled down in 1885. This left the square, 43-foot, rear-range tower to guide vessels into the harbor. Still active, its white light occults (is interrupted) briefly every four seconds.

TO SEE THE LIGHT: Swans Island can be reached via regularly scheduled ferries from Bass Harbor. For information contact the Maine State Ferry Service, P.O. Box 114, Bass Harbor, ME 04653; (207) 244–3254 or (800) 491–4883. The light is at the end of the main island road, a little less than 5 miles from the ferry slip. Services on the island are limited to a couple of small restaurants open only during summer, a general store open year-round, and a bed-and-breakfast handy for those who miss the last ferry to the mainland.

Location: Swans Island

Established: 1872

Tower height: 43 feet

Elevation of the focal plane: 105 feet

Optic: Modern

Status: Active

Characteristic: Occults every 4 seconds

Range: 9 miles

Position: 44° 08' 03
68° 26' 50

Note: Old range light tower is located nearby

ISLE AU HAUT LIGHT

This lofty, rock-strewn island is often the first land spotted by mariners emerging from the open Atlantic. In 1604 French explorer Samuel de Champlain saw its densely forested hills rising blue above the ocean horizon and gave the place its name, Isle au Haut, or "high island." Despite its beauty and the abundance of food in the rich waters surrounding the island, Champlain found no one living there. The island is still sparsely populated. Only a few dozen hardy islanders live here year-round.

The Isle au Haut Light has served the island's scatter of resident watermen since 1907. The 48-foot granite-and-brick tower rises from the rocks at the edge of the tide line on the island's Robinson Point. Still active, its light flashes red every four seconds. Nowadays the keeper's dwelling offers bed-and-breakfast rooms to island visitors in search of a truly unique experience.

TO SEE THE LIGHT: Much of pristine Isle au Haut is part of Acadia National Park. Ferries from Stonington provide passenger access to the island; call (207) 367–6516. For rooms at the lighthouse, contact The Keeper's House, P.O. Box 26, Isle au Haut, ME 04645; (207) 367–2261.

Location: Isle au Haut

Established: 1907

Tower height: 48 feet

Elevation of the focal plane: 48 feet

Optic: Modern (solar powered)

Status: Active

Characteristic: Flashes red every 4 seconds

Range: 8 miles

Position: 44° 03' 54 68° 39' 06

Note: Now a delightful bed-and-breakfast

CHAPTER TWO
THE MIDDLE COAST: FROM PENOBSCOT BAY TO BOOTHBAY HARBOR

Travelers have visited the mid-coast of Maine and marveled at the beauty of its stony sea cliffs and thickly forested hillsides since long before there was such a thing as a summer vacation. Nowadays, countless warm weather getaways are spent in Maine, which as anyone who reads license plates knows, is called the "Vacation State." Most tourists who come to Maine spend much of their time on its rocky mid-coast, and why shouldn't they? There's great food, including some of the best lobster on the planet, plenty of sailing, kayaking, hiking, and fishing, and lots to see. Antique towns and villages, such as Boothbay Harbor, Rockland, Camden, and Castine attract hordes of summertime visitors.

Far less accessible to tourists, though nonetheless popular, are the mid-coast's numerous historic light stations. Some, such as the Pemaquid Point Light, south of Waldoboro, attract more than their share of visitors, while others such as those on Matinicus Rock or Eagle Island are rarely seen at all. Certainly among the most remote of them is the Saddleback Ledge Light located on a barren scrap of exposed granite near the southeastern entrance of Penobscot Bay.

Today travelers are likely to see the Saddleback Ledge tower only from the air or from the deck of a passing excursion vessel, but for some lighthouse keepers, the ledge was far more than a distant vision—it was home. Until the beacon on Saddleback Ledge was automated in 1954, keepers had to live here year-round in order to keep the light burning and warn mariners. For years at a time, no one but keepers set foot on Saddleback. During the 1930s, however, the station received quite an extraordinary visit—from a flock of suicidal ducks. Old-time Saddleback Ledge keeper W. W. Wells told the following story.

Lighthouse Attacked by Ducks

We keepers were setting in the kitchen talking about the [First] World War when bang, bang, bang, something came against the windowpanes. We thought that another war had started that we had not heard about. I heard glass smash in the lantern, and with this I thought sure the enemy were trying to extinguish the light.

This was just around supper time. Darkness had come on
and with it came all the evidence that we were going to get a
Sou'easter. As the storm struck so did the cannonading. I
could not help thinking that it was only fair to inform us of the
attack that was about to be made. A war with Mexico and
Japan seemed to be the last topic of conversation just before
the unexpected arrived. But who wanted to blow up a friendly
old lighthouse that always did good instead of harm, and
which mariners who sailed their ships along the coast loved
and respected. Crash! And a bird came sailing through a
pane of glass, dropping at my feet.

He began fluttering around the floor with one wing bro-
ken, and his bill telescoped almost through his head. He did
not live long. In came another and away went another win-
dowpane. The phenomenon was repeated again and again
until the birds began to pile up like a mound.

Just when I thought the cannonading had ceased, one
big sea drake struck the plate glass in the tower lantern and
came through without asking for a transfer. When he struck
he broke up the works. Before he stopped he put out the light
and broke prisms out of the lens. The bird weighed over ten
pounds.

Saddleback in darkness, what would the people think on
land and sea? Only those who live in lighthouses could realize
what excitement it all caused. The keepers got right to work,
first to get the light going and then to make repairs as fast as
possible. It was not long before old Saddleback was throwing
her beams again as if nothing had ever happened.

One of us went to step out in the gallery when a big sea
duck reported with bayonet and charged so heavily as to
knock one's feet out from under. There was no more taking
any chances leaving the kitchen until silence told the keepers
that the enemy had retreated. When all had quieted down it
was a strange sight that the keepers were greeted with, for at
the base of the tower was a tremendous heap of birds, some
dead and others alive. Those that were just dazed and
needed to recuperate we placed in the boathouse, and the
next day they went on their way.

SADDLEBACK LEDGE LIGHT

Location: Near Isle au Haut

Established: 1839

Tower height: 42 feet

Elevation of the focal plane: 54 feet

Optic: Modern

Status: Active

Characteristic: Flashes every 6 seconds

Range: 9 miles

Position: 44° 00' 54 68° 43' 36

Note: Exceptionally remote and isolated

Saddleback Ledge, near Isle au Haut, is a bare scrap of rock exposed on all sides to the pounding sea. A 42-foot, cone-shaped stone tower has guarded the ledge since 1839, its flashing white light warning sailors of the certain calamity that awaits them if they come too close. The lighthouse was automated in 1954, but until that time, keepers who had little or no contact with the outside world for weeks or even months at a stretch kept vigil here. Although the tower still clings precariously to the barren rock, all traces of dwellings and outbuildings have been swept away by wind, water, and time.

TO SEE THE LIGHT: The Saddleback Ledge Light is a prominent feature of almost any cruise traversing the eastern approaches to Maine's impressive Penobscot Bay. Both two-day and week-long schooner cruises are available in Camden, Rockport, and Rockland, Maine; (800) 807–9463. These cruises may or may not pass by Saddleback Ledge, but more than a few lighthouses will be on the itinerary.

DEER ISLAND THOROUGHFARE LIGHT

Ronald J. Foster

All that remains of this pre-Civil War light station is the 25-foot square brick tower on Mark Island, now a wildlife refuge. The light remains active, however, and guides fishing boats and pleasure craft into the thoroughfare that links Stonington to the Atlantic. A plastic lens now serves in place of the original fourth-order Fresnel.

TO SEE THE LIGHT: The light can be seen from the heights above Stonington, as authentic and hardworking a fishing village as you'll likely see anywhere along the Maine coast. While in town, stop in for some chowder at the Fisherman's Friend restaurant. Summer sightseeing cruises from Stonington often pass by the tower; call (207) 367–6516.

Location: Near Stonington

Established: 1857

Tower height: 25 feet

Elevation of the focal plane: 52 feet

Optic: Modern (solar powered)

Status: Active

Characteristic: Flashes every 6 seconds

Range: 6 miles

Position: 44° 08' 00 68° 31' 30

Note: Rare bald eagles and eider ducks nest nearby

EAGLE ISLAND LIGHT

First lit in 1838 during the presidential administration of Martin Van Buren, the Eagle Island Light still guides vessels around Hardhead Shoals and into Penobscot Bay. One of a chain of lights near the mouth of the Penobscot River, including those at Dice Head and Fort Point, it marked a clear path through the rocky bay for a host of nineteenth-century freighters carrying lumber from mills in Bucksport and Bangor.

The short, whitewashed rubble-stone tower stands on a grassy cliff that helps elevate its light to more than 100 feet above high tide. A fourth-order Fresnel lens that previously served here was removed in 1963 in favor of an automated plastic lens. The 1,200-pound brass fog bell was decommissioned at the same time, but not in a manner the Coast Guard might have hoped. It broke away, rolled over the cliff, and fell into the sea. A lobsterman later salvaged the huge bell and sold it to noted nature photographer Eliot Porter for use as a dinner bell.

TO SEE THE LIGHT: Eagle Island Light is best seen from the water. Summer schooner cruises may pass the island (see travel information for Saddleback Ledge Light). Keep in mind that Maine has several Eagle Islands. This one is in Penobscot Bay. The one in Casco Bay, near Portland, was the home of Admiral Robert E. Peary, the first man to reach the North Pole.

Location: Eagle Island

Established: 1838

Tower height: 30 feet

Elevation of the focal plane: 106 feet

Optic: Modern (solar powered)

Status: Active

Characteristic: Flashes every 4 seconds

Range: 9 miles

Position: 44° 13' 04 68° 46' 04

Note: Original 1838 tower still serves

DICE HEAD LIGHT

📠 🚉 📷

Location: Castine

Established: 1829

Tower height: 51 feet
(old tower)

Elevation of the focal
plane: 27 feet (metal
tower)

Optic: Modern

Status: Active (on nearby
metal tower)

Characteristic: Flashes
every 6 seconds

Range: 11 miles

Position: 44° 22' 54
68° 49' 12

Note: Serves one of the
oldest communities in
America

One of America's most historic small towns, Castine traces its beginnings to a French fur-trading station established in 1614. Seafaring nations long coveted the rocky heights above Dice Head, which dominates the entrance to the Penobscot River. Over the years the flags of four nations fluttered above forts here, and several battles were fought for possession of the town.

In 1829 the Lighthouse Service built a rubble-stone-and-brick tower high up on the cliffs of Dice Head to guide lumber ships in and out of the Penobscot. The light also welcomed home the clipper ships of Castine captains on the last leg of adventurous trading cruises that took them as far away as China. A colonial Cape dwelling, added to the station in 1858, was attached to the tower by a short, enclosed passageway. At the same time the original Winslow Lewis lamp-and-reflector system was replaced with a fourth-order Fresnel lens. Its powerful beacon could penetrate 17 miles of storm-tossed Penobscot Bay waters.

The Coast Guard discontinued the lighthouse in 1956, replacing it with a flashing beacon shining from a small iron tower located on the rocks beneath the cliffs. Badly damaged by fire in 1999, the dwelling has been repaired.

TO SEE THE LIGHT: Anyone who appreciates history, old homes, and matchless ocean scenery will love Castine. To get there, turn off U.S. Highway 1 at Orland and follow Routes 175 and 166 to the town. The light is at the end of Battle Avenue. The lighthouse itself is a private residence and not open to the public.

| # FORT POINT LIGHT

📷 🚻 🖼

Location: Stockton Springs

Established: 1836

Tower height: 31 feet

Elevation of the focal plane: 88 feet

Optic: Fresnel (fourth order)

Status: Active

Characteristic: Fixed white

Range: 15 miles

Position: 44° 28' 00
68° 48' 42

Note: Near the site of an eighteenth-century fort

During the nineteenth century as many as 200 lumber ships might have passed the square-towered Fort Point Light in a single day. Established in 1836 by order of President Andrew Jackson, the light pointed the way to the Penobscot River and beyond to Bangor, at that time the world's busiest lumber port.

Although not much taller than the attached keeper's dwelling, the 31-foot tower stands on a high promontory, its light 88 feet above the water. The lantern still contains the fourth-order Fresnel lens installed when the station was renovated in 1857. A pyramid-shaped fog-bell house stands nearby, one of the last of its kind.

TO SEE THE LIGHT: Turn off U.S. Highway 1 in Stockton Springs and follow East Cape Road to Fort Point State Park and the light. Park employees occupy the dwelling, but visitors may walk the grounds and enjoy a sweeping view of the Penobscot Bay. Nearby are the ruins of Fort Pownall, where British and American forces fought two battles during the Revolutionary War.

GOOSE ROCKS LIGHT

The Fox Island Thoroughfare separates Vinalhaven Island from the smaller North Haven Island and provides a shortcut for vessels passing between the east and west Penobscot Bay channels. A killer ledge lurks just beneath the surface of this otherwise inviting passage. Since 1890 the ledge has been marked by an open-water light tower built atop an iron and concrete caisson. The 51-foot cast-iron tower resembles the Lubec Channel "sparkplug" Light, about a hundred miles to the east. It is difficult to imagine that keepers once lived and worked in this confined space. Automated since 1963, the solar-powered beacon flashes red every six seconds.

TO SEE THE LIGHT: The offshore tower can be seen from Calderwood Point on Vinalhaven Island, but is best seen by boat. Summer cruises to this and other lighthouses in this area are available in Camden; call (800) 223–5459 or (207) 236–4404.

Location: Vinalhaven

Established: 1890

Tower height: 51 feet

Elevation of the focal plane: 51 feet

Optic: Modern (solar powered)

Status: Active

Characteristic: Flashes red every 6 seconds

Range: 12 miles

Position: 44° 08' 08 68° 49' 50

Note: Built on an open-water caisson

GRINDLE POINT LIGHT

📠 🚪

Location: Islesboro

Established: 1850

Tower height: 39 feet

Elevation of the focal
plane: 39 feet

Optic: Modern

Status: Active

Characteristic: Flashes
green every 4 seconds

Range: 5 miles

Position: 44° 16' 54
68° 56' 36

Note: Reactivated in
1987 after half a century
of disuse

William G. Kaufhold

A narrow blade of rock more than 10 miles long cleaves the
upper reaches of Penobscot Bay. Known as Islesboro, it is the
summer home to many wealthy out-of-staters (known to locals
as "people from away") as well as a community of Maine fishing
folk. Most residents travel to and from the mainland via a car ferry
that crosses over from Lincolnville several times each day. A small
brick lighthouse marks the Islesboro ferry landing.

The square, 39-foot brick tower, built in 1874, replaced an earlier lighthouse in operation since 1850. The station was decommissioned in 1934. Under pressure from local traditionalists, however,
the Coast Guard reactivated the old lighthouse in 1987. Residents
and visitors can see its flashing green light from several points
along U.S. Highway 1 near Lincolnville.

TO SEE THE LIGHT: The Islesboro ferry schedule varies, with only two
daily round-trip crossings from January through May, up to seven
each day during summer, and three or more daily from September
through December. Contact the Maine State Ferry Service, P.O.
Box 214, Lincolnville, ME 04849; (207) 734–6935. The light
stands adjacent to the ferry slip. The Sailor's Memorial Museum,
open daily in July and August, is located in the keeper's dwelling.

CURTIS ISLAND LIGHT

During summer passenger schooners with masts taller and stouter than telephone poles crowd Camden's harbor and lend this charming coastal town a distinctly nineteenth-century feeling. On their way into the harbor, the schooners pass Curtis Island, with its tiny brick light tower and compact clapboard keeper's dwelling. The squat tower, only 25 feet tall, was built in 1896 to replace an earlier structure that had served for sixty years. The original fourth-order Fresnel lens remains in place. Its fixed green light is now solar powered.

TO SEE THE LIGHT: Located on the far side of the heavily forested island, the light is almost impossible to see from land. Harbor cruises often swing around the island so that their passengers can glimpse the little tower and dwelling. A range of granite mountains meets the sea at Camden, and visitors should definitely set aside time to enjoy the town and its picturesque setting. Several of Camden's schooners offer extended cruises, with ample opportunities to view and photograph Maine lighthouses. For more information on Camden or its schooners, call the Camden Chamber of Commerce at (207) 236–4404.

Location: Camden

Established: 1835

Tower height: 25 feet

Elevation of the focal plane: 52 feet

Optic: Modern (solar powered)

Status: Active

Characteristic: Green occulting every 4 seconds

Range: 8 miles

Position: 42° 12' 06
69° 02' 54

Note: A favorite of schooner passengers

ROCKLAND BREAKWATER LIGHT

During the nineteenth century, prodigious quantities of lime and construction stone were shipped through the appropriately named port of Rockland, Maine. Freighters lying at anchor in Rockland's unprotected harbor were often at the mercy of high waves rolling in from the sea. To offset this danger the government built a breakwater in 1888, marking its outer end with a small trapezoidal light tower. In 1902 both breakwater and harbor signal were updated. Engineers extended the breakwater to its present length of more than a mile and constructed a more substantial lighthouse to warn mariners of its presence.

The station's square, 25-foot tower rises from the corner of its two-story dwelling. The light stands on a platform of squared-off granite blocks. A modern optic now does the work of the fourth-order Fresnel lens that formerly produced its flashing white light.

TO SEE THE LIGHT: From U.S. Highway 1 in Rockland follow Waldo
Road and Samoset Road to the Marie Reed Breakwater Park.
Visitors can hike out the breakwater to the light. The lighthouse and
its light, often stunning at night, also can be seen from points along
the Rockland waterfront. Lighthouse lovers have another treat in
store at Rockland. The Maine Lighthouse Museum on Park Drive
houses the most astounding collection of lighthouse lenses and
equipment anywhere in America. This delightful and highly informa-
tive museum focuses on lighthouse history and engineering.
Contact the Maine Lighthouse Museum, 1 Park Drive, Rockland,
ME 04841; (207) 594–3301.

Location: Rockland

Established: 1888

Tower height: 25 feet

Elevation of the focal
plane: 39 feet

Optic: Modern

Status: Active

Characteristic: Flashes
every 5 seconds

Range: 17 miles

Position: 44° 06' 15
69° 04' 39

Note: Listed on the
National Register of
Historic Places

OWLS HEAD LIGHT

Ferry passengers leaving Rockland often scan the headland at the mouth of the harbor, looking for its legendary owl. Anyone with a good imagination can see the old owl sculpted by nature into the rocks. A far more obvious feature of the promontory, however, is the short, white cylinder of its lighthouse. Built in 1825, this little lighthouse is beloved by mariners who, for the better part of two centuries, have followed its fixed white beacon to the safety of Rockland Harbor. The classic fourth-order Fresnel lens that has long served the station remains in place.

The station's especially powerful fog signal has also kept countless ships from crashing on the rocks. Spot, the family dog of a keeper who worked here during the 1930s, is credited with having saved more than a few fog-blinded mariners with his ceaseless barking. What is more, the keeper trained the clever mutt to pull on the fog-bell rope whenever his sharp ears heard a vessel approaching.

TO SEE THE LIGHT: From Rockland take North Shore Road and follow signs to Owls Head State Park. From the parking area a short drive along a highly scenic access road leads to the light. Keep in mind that this is an active Coast Guard facility. Also, be prepared to hold your ears, as the fog signal is so powerful it can damage hearing. The lighthouse can also be seen and enjoyed from the Vinalhaven ferry. For information, call (207) 596–2203.

Location: Rockland

Established: 1825

Tower height: 30 feet

Elevation of the focal plane: 100 feet

Optic: Fresnel (fourth order)

Status: Active

Characteristic: Fixed white

Range: 16 miles

Position: 44° 05' 30 69° 02' 36

Note: Marks the entrance to Rockland Harbor

BROWNS HEAD LIGHT

The Browns Head Light began marking the western approaches to Vinalhaven Island when Andrew Jackson was president. Completed in 1832 at a cost of only $4,000—including the adjacent dwelling—the 20-foot stone tower became a permanent feature of the island landscape. To this day its fixed white light guides fishing boats and ferries. In 1902 the government strengthened the beacon by exchanging the existing fifth-order Fresnel lens for a more powerful fourth-order Fresnel, which remains in service.

TO SEE THE LIGHT: The Rockland/Vinalhaven ferries make three trips each way daily from April through October and twice daily during the rest of the year. The 15-mile crossing takes about seventy minutes. For ferry information contact the Maine State Ferry Service, P.O. Box 645, Rockland, ME 04841; (207) 596–2203. The light station is 6 miles north of Vinalhaven Village and about a mile off North Haven Road. The more than century-old dwelling is now a private residence. While in Vinalhaven, don't miss the Historical Society Museum, which features the original Browns Head fog bell. Of particular interest to lighthouse lovers is Armbrust Hill, just south of the village. From here you can see the towers at Matinicus Island to the southwest and Two Bush Island and Saddleback Ledge to the southeast.

Location: Vinalhaven

Established: 1832

Tower height: 20 feet

Elevation of the focal plane: 39 feet

Optic: Fresnel (fourth order)

Status: Active

Characteristic: Fixed white

Range: 14 miles

Position: 44° 06' 42 68° 54' 36

Note: Vinalhaven town manager lives in the keeper's residence

HERON NECK LIGHT

Among the approximately one thousand hardy souls who live year-round on Vinalhaven Island, a considerable number are fishermen. Just as their forefathers have for nearly one and a half centuries, these mariners depend on the light at Heron Neck to guide them into Carver's Harbor. Its fixed white and red beacon

marks the entrance to Hurricane Sound as well as the approaches to Vinalhaven. A fifth-order Fresnel lens beamed out from atop the 30-foot tower until replaced by a plastic lens in 1982. The Island Institute now owns the station and surrounding property, located on Green Island, just off the main island of Vinalhaven. A nonprofit organization, the institute is dedicated to preserving Maine's old maritime culture. Severely damaged by fire in 1989, the old keeper's residence was handsomely restored with funds supplied by a private donor.

TO SEE THE LIGHT: This light is very difficult to reach, but it can be seen from boats approaching Vinalhaven Island or entering Hurricane Sound. Summer cruises from Rockland or Stonington often feature views of the Heron Neck, Goose Rocks, or Browns Head Lights. For information and advice on these and other Maine attractions, call (800) 533–9595.

Location: Vinalhaven

Established: 1853

Tower height: 30 feet

Elevation of the focal plane: 92 feet

Optic: Modern

Status: Active

Characteristic: Fixed red

Range: 13 miles

Position: 44° 01' 30
68° 51' 44

Note: Fire-damaged dwelling has been restored

TWO BUSH ISLAND LIGHT

L ong ago, seamen heading north toward the west side of the Penobscot Bay scanned the horizon for a small island, barren except for a pair of scraggly pines. They knew that "Two Bush" Island marked a safe channel leading into the bay. In 1897 the government gave them a more substantial marker by building a 42-foot-tall, square brick light tower on the island.

For many years a fifth-order Fresnel lens served here, but in 1963 a modern optic was installed, and the station was automated. Later, a U.S. Army Special Forces team blew up the old keeper's dwelling as part of a training exercise. The tower still stands, however, and its light remains active, flashing white and red every five seconds. Its beacon can be seen from up to 17 miles away.

TO SEE THE LIGHT: Often passengers can see Two Bush Island Light or its beacon from the Vinalhaven ferry or the decks of summer excursion boats headed for Matinicus Island or other coastal attractions. For ferry schedules and prices, call (207) 596–2203. For information on cruises call the Maine Visitors Bureau at (800) 533–9595.

Location: Near Rockland

Established: 1897

Tower height: 42 feet

Elevation of the focal plane: 65 feet

Optic: Modern

Status: Active

Characteristic: Flashes every 5 seconds

Range: 17 miles

Position: 43° 57' 51
69° 04' 26

Note: Marks the entrance to Penobscot Bay

Two Bush Island Light as it stood before the 1970 Green Beret demolition exercise that destroyed the keeper's house. Only the square light tower remains. U.S. Coast Guard

MATINICUS ROCK LIGHT

📷 📷

Location: Near Matinicus
Island south of Rockland

Established: 1827

Tower height: 48 feet

Elevation of the focal
plane: 90 feet

Optic: Modern (solar
powered)

Status: Active

Characteristic: flashes
every 10 seconds

Range: 20 miles

Position: 43° 47' 00
68° 51' 18

Note: Lighthouse heroine
Abbie Burgess lived here

Exposed to rain, wind, fog, and giant waves, Matinicus Rock seems an unlikely place to build a lighthouse of wood, but that is exactly what the Lighthouse Service did, throwing up two flimsy wooden towers in 1827. Surprisingly, the wooden towers survived almost twenty years; not until 1846 were they replaced by a pair of granite towers.

The new towers stood 60 yards apart, and, like their predecessors, they displayed two lights that appeared quite close together when seen from a distance. The builders hoped mariners could easily distinguish these key beacons from others along this especially dangerous portion of the Maine coast. Unfortunately, the Winslow Lewis lamps and reflectors used in these towers proved too weak for the station to serve its purpose effectively.

In 1857 the Lighthouse Board ordered the station's towers rebuilt and outfitted with third-order Fresnel lenses. Built with massive granite blocks, these towers have stood up to the worst the sea could throw at them for nearly one and a half centuries. Although the south tower still stands, it lost its job in 1924, when the Lighthouse Service decided to stop using twin lights and removed its lantern and lens. The north light still shines, warning mariners away from the rock with powerful white flashes, visible every ten seconds from up to 20 miles away. The north tower's old Fresnel was replaced by a plastic lens in 1983.

TO SEE THE LIGHT: The Fresnel lens from the old south tower can be seen at the excellent Maine Lighthouse

Museum, 1 Park Drive, Rockland, ME 04841; (207) 594–3301.
Excursions to Matinicus Rock are available during summer from
Rockland. For information on available cruises, call the Maine
Visitors Bureau at (800) 533–9595. The island is a favorite of bird-
watchers since it is home to puffins, petrels, and other rare
seabirds. The old light station is a favorite of history buffs since this
is where heroic teenager Abbie Burgess helped save her family and
pet chickens during a tremendous storm in 1856 (see Introduction).

WHITEHEAD LIGHT

📷 🖼

Location: On Sprucehead Island near Thomaston

Established: 1807

Tower height: 41 feet

Elevation of the focal plane: 75 feet

Optic: Modern

Status: Active

Characteristic: Green occulting every 4 seconds

Range: 6 miles

Position: 43° 58' 43 69° 07' 27

Note: Abbie Burgess served here with her husband Isaac Grant

Established by order of President Thomas Jefferson in 1807, this is one of the oldest light stations in Maine. The 41-foot granite tower and adjacent wooden dwelling date from 1852 when a third-order Fresnel lens replaced an outmoded lamp-and-reflector system. A 2,000-pound fog bell once served here. For many years it was rung by a mechanical contraption powered by the waves. Abbie (Burgess) Grant and her husband Isaac Grant were among the more than eighty keepers and assistants who served here from 1807 until the station was automated in 1982, when its classic lens was replaced by a modern optic. The lens that served here for more than a century is now on display at the Shore Village Museum in Rockland.

Having guarded the southern entrance to Maine's Penobscot Bay for nearly two centuries, the Whitehead Light station on Pine Island remains an active aid to navigation. While the Coast Guard maintains the station's light and fog signal, a private children's camp leases the keeper's house and other station property.

TO SEE THE LIGHT: The tower can be viewed from the end of Sprucehead Point Road in Sprucehead, but is best seen from the water. Also visible from Sprucehead is the Two Bush Island Light (1897). However, the 42-foot Two Bush tower is located several miles offshore and is best seen from the water. The Maine Lighthouse Museum address is 1 Park Drive, Rockland, ME 04841; (207) 594–3301.

Jeremy D'Entremont

B uilt in 1857, the Tenants Harbor Lighthouse, southwest of Rockland, Maine, guided fishing boats and other vessels for more than seventy-five years. When the station was closed in 1933, its wooden cape dwelling and attached 27-foot brick tower were sold to private owners. For years, it has been owned by the family of the famous artist Andrew Wyeth, who is said to have painted some of his best work while living here. Wyeth's son Jamie, also an artist, now lives and paints in the keeper's dwelling.

TO SEE THE LIGHT: The lighthouse is on private property, but it can be seen from the water as well as from a landing off Route 131 in Tenants Harbor.

Location: Tenants Harbor

Established: 1857

Tower height: 27 feet

Status: Deactivated in 1933

Note: Artist Andrew Wyeth once lived here

MARSHALL POINT LIGHT

The small stone light on Marshall Point serves Port Clyde, one of the loveliest and most bucolic fishing villages in America. Built in 1858, the signal replaced an earlier soapstone structure that had stood here since 1832. Rising from the water's edge, the 30-foot tower looks much like the one at Isle au Haut with its upper section of brick and lower one of granite blocks. A wooden walkway at one time provided access to shore. A fifth-order Fresnel lens served here until 1980; now a modern optic sends out a fixed white light that can be seen from approximately 7 miles away.

TO SEE THE LIGHT: This old tower is highly recommended for lighthouse lovers because of its peaceful setting and proximity to the Marshall Point Lighthouse Museum. Managed by the St. George Historical Society, this fine little museum displays artifacts and recounts the histories of the Marshall Point, Whitehead, Tenants Harbor, and St. George Lighthouses. The museum is free and open to the public May through October. Contact the Marshall Point Lighthouse Museum, P.O. Box 247, Port Clyde, ME 04855; (207) 372–6450. The tower and museum are located at the end of Marshall Point Road in Port Clyde. Reach them via Route 131 from U.S. Highway 1 in Thomaston. On the way to Port Clyde, stop in Tenants Harbor for a look at the Tenants Harbor Lighthouse. Decommissioned in 1933, it has served as both a home and art studio of Andrew and Jamie Wyeth.

Location: Port Clyde

Established: 1832

Tower height: 30 feet

Elevation of the focal plane: 30 feet

Optic: Modern

Status: Active

Characteristic: Fixed white

Range: 7 miles

Position: 43° 55' 00
              69° 15' 42

Note: Featured in the movie *Forrest Gump* and the children's book *Nellie the Lighthouse Dog*

The unusual striated rock formations of Pemaquid Point look like ocean waves turned to stone—more than a few vessels lost in the fog have sailed up onto them with disastrous results. Established in 1827, the Pemaquid Point Light has prevented many such wrecks. Built during the administration of John Quincy Adams, the stone tower had walls 3 feet thick. Despite their bulk the original walls did not stand up to the harsh local weather and had to be rebuilt in 1835 and again in 1857. The keeper's stone dwelling also suffered and was replaced in 1857 by the wood-frame cape that nowadays houses an excellent museum.

The 38-foot tower stands high on the rocks, placing the focal point of the light almost 80 feet above sea level. The station still employs its venerable fourth-order Fresnel lens; its flashing white light can be seen some 15 miles away.

TO SEE THE LIGHT: From U.S. Highway 1 at Damariscotta follow Route 130 for 16 miles to the light. The keeper's dwelling now houses the Fisherman's Museum. The massive bronze fog bell from the old Manna Island station hangs outside. Contact the Fisherman's Museum, Pemaquid Point Road, New Harbor, ME 04554; (207) 677–2494. Cruises from nearby New Harbor pass by the active Franklin Island Lighthouse (1805) to the east of Pemaquid Point; call (800) 278–3346.

Location: Near Damariscotta

Established: 1827

Tower height: 38 feet

Elevation of the focal plane: 79 feet

Optic: Fresnel (fourth order)

Status: Active

Characteristic: Flashes every 6 seconds

Range: 15 miles

Position: 43° 50' 12
69° 30' 21

Note: Home of Fisherman's Museum

RAM ISLAND LIGHT

Located on rocky Ram Island, this light marks one of the key passages leading to Boothbay Harbor, now a popular summertime tourist destination. When the station was established in 1883, the seaside villages hereabouts were frequented mostly by fishermen. To help them avoid the ledges near the island, the government built a 35-foot granite and brick tower and fitted it with a fourth-order Fresnel lens. Keepers lived in an L-shaped residence some distance inland. Although the station was automated many years ago, both the dwelling and tower remain standing. The Fresnel lens has been replaced by a modern optic, but the beacon is still in operation. It warns mariners with an alternating red light.

Location: near Boothbay
Harbor

Established: 1883

Tower height: 35 feet

Elevation of the focal
plane: 36 feet

Optic: Modern

Status: Active

Characteristic: Alternates
red or white every 6
seconds

Range: 11 miles

Position: 43° 48' 14
69° 35' 57

Note: A favorite
of summer cruise
passengers

William G. Kaufhold

TO SEE THE LIGHT: The light can be seen from several parking areas along the shore road on Ocean Point at the end of Route 96 south of Boothbay Harbor. The Maine Maritime Museum in Bath operates summer cruises that pass Ram Island and other lighthouses along the mid-coast of Maine; call (207) 443–1316. For whale-watching cruises that pass this light call or (207) 633–3244 or (800) 636–3244.

Bob and Sandra Shanklin,
The Lighthouse People

HENDRICKS HEAD LIGHT

Location: Boothbay
Harbor

Established: 1829

Tower height: 40 feet

**Elevation of the focal
plane:** 43 feet

Optic: Modern

Status: Active

Characteristic: Fixed
white with red sector

Range: 9 miles

Position: 43° 49' 24
69° 41' 24

Note: Reactivated in 1951
after 15 years of disuse

During an especially severe storm in the late 1860s, the Hendricks Head keeper pulled an ice-encrusted mattress from the waves. Inside, the astonished man found a crying baby and a note from a sinking schooner's desperate captain who had committed his tiny daughter "into God's hands." The keeper and his wife adopted the little girl, the lost ship's only survivor.

Established in 1829, the Hendricks Head Light no doubt helped prevent many other such losses. The present 40-foot, Federal-style brick tower and connected wooden dwelling were built in 1875 on the site of the original lighthouse, destroyed by fire earlier that year. The station's automated plastic lens displays a fixed white light with red sectors.

TO SEE THE LIGHT: From U.S. Highway 1 take Route 27 through Boothbay Harbor to Southport Island. The light can be seen from a public beach just off Beach Road. Visitors can see the Burnt Island Lighthouse (1857), with its flashing red light, from the waterfront in Boothbay Harbor and, in the distance, the Cuckolds Light, dating from the early 1900s. The Ram Island Light (1883), which resembles those at Isle au

Haut and Marshall Point, can be seen from roadside overlooks
along Route 96 in Ocean Point to the east of Boothbay Harbor.
Cuckolds Light can also be seen from here. For cruises that pass
this light call (207) 633–3244 or (800) 636–3244.

Hendricks Head Light still has its old fog-bell building, which can be accessed by an elevated
walkway.

CUCKOLDS LIGHT

Jeremy D'Entremont

Location: near Boothbay
Harbor

Established: 1907

Tower height: 48 feet

Elevation of the focal
plane: 59 feet

Optic: Modern

Status: active

Characteristic: Flashes
twice every 6 seconds

Range: 12 miles

Position: 43° 46' 48
69° 39' 00

Note: Residence
destroyed in a blizzard

This mid-coast light marking the seaward approach to Boothbay Harbor barely resembles a "house" at all. A fog signal established here in 1892 was converted for use as a lighthouse some fifteen years later when a modest light tower was added to the original wood-and-stone structure. A nearby residence served as home for the keeper and his family until the station was automated in 1975. Three years after the residence was boarded up, it was demolished by a raging Maine blizzard. Having lost its place in the tiny Cuckold's tower to a plastic modern optic, the station's original fourth-order Fresnel is now proudly displayed at the Shore Village Museum in Rockland.

TO SEE THE LIGHT: From U.S. Highway 1 follow ME 27 through Boothbay Harbor and Newagen Center, turn southeast on ME 238, and drive about a quarter mile to the town landing. From here, the Cuckolds Light can be seen across the water at a distance of a little more than half a mile. For cruises that pass this light call (207) 633–3244 or (800) 636–3244.

MONHEGAN ISLAND LIGHT

About a dozen miles from the Maine coast, the near-solid granite mass of Monhegan Island rises out of the Atlantic, its 150-foot cliffs towering over the waves. Since the 1620s, the one-and-a-half-mile-long island has been home to a hardy maritime community, and a scattering of lobstering and fishing families still live there. Theirs is a tradition-minded community, and even now most residences have no electric power.

Located atop the cliffs, the 47-foot tower emits a light with a focal plane nearly 180 feet above the waves. From this height it can be seen more than 20 miles away. The present tower, completed in 1851, replaced an earlier lighthouse that had served the island since 1824. Until 1959 a magnificent second-order Fresnel lens focused the light.

TO SEE THE LIGHT: Excursions to Monhegan Island are available during summer from Boothbay Harbor (call 800–298–2284) or New Harbor (call 800–278–3346) and year-round from Port Clyde (call 207–372–8848). The Monhegan Museum, located in the keeper's house, is open July through September; (207) 596–7003

Location: Monhegan Island south of Port Clyde

Established: 1824

Tower height: 47 feet

Elevation of the focal plane: 178 feet

Optic: Modern (solar powered)

Status: Active

Characteristic: Flashes every 15 seconds

Range: 20 miles

Position: 43° 45' 54 69° 18' 54

Note: Serves traditional island fishing community

William G. Kaufhold

CHAPTER THREE:
DOWN PORTLAND WAY: FROM BATH TO KITTERY

It has been said that no matter how fast you travel in Maine, winter is always close behind. Perhaps that's why some tourists never go much beyond Portland. They are afraid the warm weather will run out on them, and they'll be stranded. Jokes aside, the southwestern coast of Maine in general, and the fine old city of Portland in particular, are no less wonderful than any other part of the state. The lobster is just as good here, the buildings just as quaint, the lighthouses just as beautiful, and when the autumn leaves are blown away by the first nor'easter, the weather is just as terrible.

In Maine waters, mariners fear the cold more than the deep. This is especially true in winter, when a shipwrecked sailor is far more likely to freeze to death than to drown. Seamen and fishermen in these parts dread the gales that roll in from the northeast and the blizzards that sweep down out of Canada. These storms often cause temperatures to drop so low that the salt spray from the waves pounding on the side of the ship rattles onto the deck like hail. Ice grips everything, encrusting the hulls and masts of schooners, locking up the clappers of fog bells, and obscuring the windows of lighthouses. Not surprisingly, wrecks are more common in winter than at other times. The stories of disaster and rescue told by Maine's lighthouse keepers often crackle with ice.

The Ghost Ship "Isidore"

In a graveyard at Kennebunkport is a stone bearing the name of Captain Leander Foss. The body of Captain Foss, however, does not rest anywhere near the stone. It is assumed that Foss went to Davy Jones's locker along with his handsome bark, which disappeared under strange circumstances off Cape Neddick in 1842. But some say that Foss still sails the seas as captain of the ghost ship *Isidore*.

A seaman named Thomas King was supposed to ship out with the *Isidore* when it set sail from Kennebunkport on the last day of

November 1842. But two days before the scheduled departure,
King woke up in a cold sweat from a terrible dream: a vision of a
wrecked ship and drowning sailors. King had no doubt that the vessel in his nightmare was the bark *Isidore* and that the dying men
were his fellow crewmen.

King told Foss about his ominous dream, but the old sea captain laughed at him. When Foss refused to delay the *Isidore*'s sailing, King begged to be let out of his contract and left behind.
Captain Foss reminded King that he had already received a
month's salary in advance, and told the frightened seaman, in the
plainest of language, to be aboard the *Isidore* when it pulled away
from the dock. The following night another member of the *Isidore*
crew had a disturbing dream. The sailor saw seven coffins and saw
himself in one of them. Foss heard about this second nightmare,
but having both little respect for superstition and a schedule to
keep, he made up his mind to sail first thing the next morning.

As November 30 dawned, the families and friends of the
Isidore's crew gathered at the Kennebunkport wharves to wish their
loved ones well. But a cloud of dread and gloom hung heavy over
the farewell, and there was little of the usual cheering and hat wav-
ing as the bark glided slowly out of the harbor. It soon began to
snow, and a bitterly cold wind came up out of the north to hurry the
Isidore toward the sea and into the realm of legend.

Among those who watched the *Isidore*'s masts disappear in
the snowy distance was Thomas King. He hid in the woods until he
was certain that the bark was under way. King expected his
acquaintances in town to scorch his ears for having jumped ship,
and they did. But his disgrace lasted only about one day.

On the following morning word came to Kennebunkport that
pieces of a large ship were scattered all along the shore in the
vicinity of Cape Neddick. It was the *Isidore*. There were no survivors
of the wreck, and only seven bodies washed ashore—one of them
the sailor who had dreamed about the seven coffins. The body of
Captain Foss was never found.

Imaginative residents and visitors to Maine's scenic coast have
reported many sightings of the *Isidore* during the century and a half
since the wreck. They describe a close-reefed bark and shadowy
figures who stand motionless on the deck and stare straight ahead.

SEGUIN ISLAND LIGHT

Among the oldest and most significant navigational stations in the eastern United States, Seguin Island Light stands on a rocky outcropping near the mouth of Maine's Kennebec River. Built by order of President George Washington, the light had John Polersky, an old Revolutionary War soldier, as its first keeper. The hard work and horrible weather ruined Polersky's health, and he soon died from the strain and exposure.

The light survived Polersky by many years but finally succumbed to a storm in 1820. The stone tower built in its place stood until 1857, when construction crews completed the present 53-foot granite tower on the island's highest point. The huge first-order Fresnel lens installed at that time still shines from its lofty perch 180 feet above the sea and can be seen from a distance of up to 18 miles.

TO SEE THE LIGHT: The light cannot be seen easily from land, but the Maine Maritime Museum runs regular tour boats to Seguin Island during summer. The museum is a must-see attraction for anyone interested in maritime history, shipbuilding, or lighthouses. Contact the Maine Maritime Museum, 243 Washington Street, Bath, ME 04530; (207) 443–1316. Museum guides can direct you to several small, but interesting, lighthouses along the Kennebec River. These include the Squirrel Point (1898), Perkins Island (1898), Pond Island (1855), Doubling Point (1898), and Doubling Point Range (1898) Lights. Most of them can be seen from Route 209 or side roads between Bath and Popham Beach. For additional cruises that pass Seguin Island Light call (207) 633–3244 or (800) 636–3244.

Location: Near Georgetown

Established: 1795

Tower height: 53 feet

Elevation of the focal plane: 180 feet

Optic: Fresnel (first order)

Status: Active

Characteristic: Fixed white

Range: 18 miles

Position: 43° 42' 30
69° 45' 30

Note: Station's mighty first-order Fresnel lens remains in use

DOUBLING POINT RANGE LIGHTS

These little range towers are only 21 and 13 feet tall, respectively. Rather simply constructed of wood, they were placed on Arrowsic Island in 1898, the same year the nearby Squirrel Point and Perkins Island Light Stations were built. They are the only active range lights in the state of Maine. As with other range lights, the Doubling Point beacons help mariners stay within a narrow safe channel. Pilots try to keep the two lights stacked one

atop the other. When the upper light slips out of the vertical either to the left or right, the approaching pilot steers in the opposite direction. Originally, both the small Doubling Point Range towers were equipped with fifth-order Fresnels, but these were replaced by plastic lenses when the lights were automated in 1979. The station's L-shaped wooden keeper's residence remains standing.

TO SEE THE LIGHT: From U. S. Highway 1 follow Route 127 south and turn right onto Whitmore's Landing Road. At Doubling Point Road, turn left, and proceed to the station parking lot. While the towers are not open, visitors are welcome to walk along the station boardwalk to view and photograph these unusual structures. For information on several other small Kennebec River lights contact the Maine Maritime Museum, 243 Washington Street, Bath, ME 04530; (207) 443–1316. Museum guides can direct you to several small, but interesting, lighthouses along the Kennebec River. These include the Squirrel Point (1898), Perkins Island (1898), Pond Island (1855), and Doubling Point Lighthouses (1898) as well as the Doubling Point Range Lights (1898). Most of them can be seen from Route 209 or side roads between Bath and Popham Beach.

Location: Lower Kennebec River

Established: 1898

Tower height: (rear) 21 feet (front) 13 feet

Elevation of the focal plane: (rear) 33 feet (front) 18 feet

Optic: Modern

Status: Active

Characteristic: Flashes every 4 seconds

Range: Approximately 4 miles

Position: 43° 53' 00
          69° 47' 42

Note: Key river marker

Bob and Sandra Shanklin,
The Lighthouse People

Location: Portland/
Casco Bay

Established: 1871

Tower height: 76 feet

Elevation of the focal
plane: 77 feet

Optic: Modern (solar
powered)

Status: Active

Characteristic: Flashes
red every 5 seconds

Range: 19 miles

Position: 43° 39' 21
70° 02' 12

Note: One of several
important Casco Bay
sentinels

An open ocean tower somewhat like the one at Minot's Ledge in Massachusetts, the Halfway Rock Light marks a notorious sea hazard about 10 miles from Portland, Maine's busiest seaport. Many ships caught by rocks here simply disappeared, the story of their loss never told or even known. Congress appropriated $50,000 to mark the rocks in 1869, but the station took two years to build. The 77-foot tower's massive granite blocks dovetail in such a way that the walls grow even stronger when pounded by the waves. The station remains active, its automated lens flashing a red warning that can be seen for 19 miles.

TO SEE THE LIGHT: The light can be seen in the distance from high points in the city of Portland. Perhaps the best view is from the Portland Observatory on Congress Street. Otherwise it can be viewed only from the water. The Portland area is rich in lighthouses, and harbor cruises, available mostly during summer, provide excellent views for photographing them. From cruise-boat decks you may see the Portland Breakwater Light (1875), Spring Point Ledge Light (1895), Ram Island Ledge Light (1905), and Portland Head Light (1791). For more information call Casco Bay cruises at (207) 774–7871, Eagle Tours at (207) 774–6498, Bay View Cruises at (207) 761–0496, or the Portland Visitors Center at (207) 772–4994.

RAM ISLAND LEDGE LIGHT

eginning in 1873, a beacon shining from atop a simple wooden tripod marked the dangerous Portland Ledge. It was replaced by the existing, much more substantial 72-foot granite tower in 1905. Nearly 3,000 tons of stone were used in construction of the tower. A powerful third-order Fresnel lens served here for many years, but was replaced by a modern optic when the station was automated in 1959.

TO SEE THE LIGHT: The Ram Island Ledge Light is located offshore about a quarter mile from the Portland Head Light. Follow Route 77 to Fort Williams Park, just south of South Portland.

Location: Cape Elizabeth

Established: 1873

Tower height: 72 feet

Elevation of the focal plane: 77 feet

Optic: Modern

Status: Active

Characteristic: Flashes twice every 6 seconds

Range: 8 miles

Position: 43° 37' 54
70° 11' 12

Note: Warns mariners away from a barren, wave-swept rock

PORTLAND BREAKWATER LIGHT

📑 🚗 📷

Location: South Portland

Established: 1855

Tower height: 26 feet

Elevation of the focal
plane: 30 feet

Optic: Modern

Status: Active

Characteristic: Flashes
every 4 seconds

Range: 5 miles

Position: 43° 39' 12
70° 14' 38

Note: Relit in 2002

Classical Greek styling gives this little thirteen-foot tower the look of a giant chess rook. Despite its rather whimsical appearance, the tower and its beacon were a serious concern to mariners. The light alerted them to the presence of the Portland Breakwater, at one time more than half a mile long. Built in response to a destructive storm in 1831, the breakwater was intended to protect the harbor, but since it was sometimes difficult to see, it posed a considerable threat to shipping. In 1855, a lighthouse was placed at the end of the breakwater to warn mariners. As the harbor was filled in over the years, the mainland marched steadily out toward the end of the breakwater with the result that the lighthouse now stands on dry land. The tower seen here today dates from 1875 when it replaced an earlier structure that was hauled away for use elsewhere as a watchtower. A small sixth-order Fresnel lens provided the beacon until the light was extinguished in 1942. In 2002, some sixty years after its lantern went dark, the station's beacon was relit to the delight of both mariners and history buffs.

TO SEE THE LIGHT: From Route 77 in South Portland follow Broadway, Breakwater Drive, and then Madison Street to the parking area for Bug Light Park and the light. This tower is one of several lights highlighting Portland-area sightseeing cruises; call (207) 761–0496.

Ross Tracy

Ross Tracy

SPRING POINT LEDGE LIGHT

onsisting of a cylindrical, iron tower set atop a massive caisson, the Spring Point Ledge Light is one of only a few "sparkplug" style light towers in northern New England. Resembling the ignition plugs used in gasoline or diesel engines, lights like this one are designed to survive gale-force winds, high water, and tremendous pressures placed on them by winter ice floes. The Spring Point Ledge Light has stood up to these natural forces for more than a century. Since 1897, the station's beacon has safely guided vessels past the long, low breakwater protecting Portland Harbor. The breakwater was built during the late 1800s after a series of destructive storms had played havoc with harbor facilities and vessels that had sought safety there in vain.

TO SEE THE LIGHT: From Portland, follow ME 77 across the bridge into South Portland, drive to the end of Broadway. Then take Fort Road to the Portland Harbor Museum, located beside the water and near the breakwater leading to the light. For more information on the museum and light access call (207) 799–6337. For cruises that pass the light call Casco Bay Cruises at (207) 774–7871.

Location: Portland

Established: 1897

Tower height: 54 feet

Elevation of the focal plane: 54 feet

Optic: Modern

Status: Active

Characteristic: Flashes every 6 seconds (red sectors)

Range: 14 miles

Position: 43° 39' 06 70° 13' 24

Note: Stands on massive caisson at the end of the harbor breakwater

PORTLAND HEAD LIGHT

Among its first acts the U.S. Congress created a Lighthouse Establishment in 1789. Constructing the Portland Head Light became the first major project federal lighthouse officials undertook. Its 80-foot fieldstone tower was completed in 1791, during George Washington's third year as president. Remarkably, it still stands and, despite numerous repairs and renovations over the years, looks much as it did in the late eighteenth century. A rambling, red-roofed keeper's residence stands beside the tower on a rocky, wave-swept headland. Together they form one of the most beautiful and frequently photographed scenes in the East.

The Coast Guard removed the station's fourth-order Fresnel lens in 1989, the bicentennial year of the Lighthouse Service. A modern rotating beacon serves here now, its powerful flashing light seen for up to 25 miles. The dwelling now houses the Museum at Portland Head, where visitors can see an enormous second-order bivalve lens that once served here.

TO SEE THE LIGHT: The light is located in Fort Williams Park, off Route 77 near South Portland. Contact the Museum at Portland Head, P.O. Box 6260, Cape Elizabeth, ME 04107; (207) 799–2661. Fortunate passengers of airliners landing at Portland occasionally enjoy a stunning view of Portland Head and its two-centuries-old light.

Location: South Portland

Established: 1791

Tower height: 80 feet

Elevation of the focal plane: 101 feet

Optic: Airport-style beacon

Status: Active

Characteristic: Flashes every 4 seconds

Range: 24 miles

Position: 43° 37' 24
70° 12' 30

Note: First lighthouse completed by the federal government

Ross Tracy

CAPE ELIZABETH LIGHT

The Cape Elizabeth Light station once guided mariners with two lights—one fixed, the other flashing. The twin lights, shining from towers spaced about 300 yards apart, allowed navigators approaching from any direction to quickly find their position on a chart. The first towers built here in 1828 cost the government only $4,250 and lasted for almost half a century. Finally, all but destroyed by wind, weather, and the sea, the deteriorated towers were replaced in 1874 by the handsome cast-iron towers that still stand. The Lighthouse Service stopped using twin beacons in 1924; afterward, only the east light was displayed. Although its second-order Fresnel lens was removed in 1994, the beacon remains in service, its flashing white light visible some 15 miles away.

TO SEE THE LIGHT: Together with their gorgeous setting, the 67-foot Italianate Cape Elizabeth towers make this one of the loveliest and most distinctive lighthouses in America. It is located in Two Lights State Park, easily reached from Route 77 via Two Lights Road. Keep in mind that the residence and grounds are privately owned. A visit to Cape Elizabeth can be part of a compact lighthouse adventure including nearby Portland Head and several other lighthouses in the Portland area.

Location: Cape Elizabeth

Established: 1828

Tower height: 67 feet

Elevation of the focal plane: 129 feet

Optic: Modern

Status: Active

Characteristic: Flashes 4 times every 15 seconds

Range: 15 miles

Position: 43° 34' 00
70° 12' 00

Note: Formerly displayed a double beacon and was known as "Twin Lighthouses"

WOOD ISLAND LIGHT

Bob and Sandra Shanklin,
The Lighthouse People

Location: Near Biddeford

Established: 1808

Tower height: 47 feet

Elevation of the focal
plane: 71 feet

Optic: Modern

Status: Active

Characteristic: Alternates
white and green every 10
seconds

Range: 18 miles

Position: 43° 27' 24
70° 19' 42

Note: At least fifty
keepers served at this
station

Among the oldest light stations in Maine, the Wood Island Light first shined in 1808 during the administration of President Thomas Jefferson. The original structures have all been replaced, but the existing ones are nonetheless quite venerable—the granite tower dates from 1839, while the wooden keeper's residence dates from before the Civil War. These wonderful old buildings became to deteriorate after the station was automated in 1986. Fortunately, they have been saved and are being restored, thanks largely to the efforts of local preservationists and support from the American Lighthouse Foundation headquartered in nearby Wells, Maine.

TO SEE THE LIGHT: The light can be seen distantly from points along the shore near Biddeford. From Route 9, follow ME 238 (Bridge Road), turn left at a T-intersection, and park near Ocean Avenue. Walk through a closed vehicular gate and proceed about a quarter mile to a viewing area. The Friends of the Wood Island Lighthouse manages the property and offers occasional tours; www.wood islandlighthouse.org

BOON ISLAND LIGHT

The Boon Island story reaches back at least as far as 1710 when a hapless British vessel known as the *Nottingham* galley wrecked on its jagged rocks. Those who survived the wreck suffered great privation, and their tale is related in the classic novel *Boon Island* by Kenneth Roberts. To save other ships from a similar fate, a light was established on this extraordinarily remote and rugged island in 1799, the same year George Washington died (Washington was the father not just of the United States but also of the U.S. Lighthouse Service).

Of the more than fifty keepers who served here, Thomas Henry Orcutt lasted the longest. Arriving in 1886, Orcutt tended the light until 1905, a stretch of nineteen years.

The original Boon Island Lighthouse consisted of a modest wooden tower and rustic dwelling. Several other towers were built here before 1855, when the existing granite structure was completed. More than 130 feet tall, it is an impressive building and one of the tallest light towers in New England.

TO SEE THE LIGHT: Although the light can be seen at a distance from Cape Neddick, close-up views are available only from the air or water. For cruises that approach the island, call (800) 441–4620.

Location: Boon Island near York

Established: 1799

Tower height: 133 feet

Elevation of the focal plane: 137 feet

Optic: Modern (solar powered)

Status: Active

Characteristic: Flashes every 5 seconds

Range: 19 miles

Position: 43° 07' 18
70° 28' 36

Note: More than fifty keepers tended this light

Ronald J. Foster

CAPE NEDDICK LIGHT

Just off Cape Neddick, near the old colonial town of York, Maine, lies a small, barren island long known to local fishermen as the "Nubble." Imaginative visitors say they can see the ghostly likenesses of people—perhaps sailors shipwrecked here long ago—in the fantastic shapes of the island's rock formations. Since 1879,

the Cape Neddick Light, stationed on the island's highest point, has warned mariners of the deadly Nubble. From a 40-foot cast-iron tower, its flashing red light signals danger. A wood-frame residence connects to the tower by a covered walkway. Delightful miniature lighthouses decorate the balusters of the service gallery.

TO SEE THE LIGHT: From U.S. Highway 1 take Route 1A into York Beach. Turn right and follow Nubble Road to Nubble Point to enjoy a fine view of the light. Do not attempt to walk across to the island; the footing is dangerous, and tides may strand you. While in the area, don't miss the Lighthouse Depot in Wells, several miles north of York. This

---

Location: York

Established: 1879

Tower height: 41 feet

Elevation of the focal plane: 88 feet

Optic: Fresnel (fourth order)

Status: Active

Characteristic: Blinks red every 6 seconds

Range: 13 miles

Position: 43° 09' 54 70° 35' 30

Note: Delightful architecture

extraordinary shop is a treasure house of information and keep-
sakes related to Cape Neddick and lighthouses throughout the
United States. Write to Lighthouse Depot, P.O. Box 427, Wells, ME
04090; or call (207) 646–3128. For mail orders call (800)
758–1444.

Ross Tracy

WHALEBACK LEDGE LIGHT

📷 📠

Location: Kittery Point

Established: 1820

Tower height: 50 feet

Elevation of the focal plane: 59 feet

Optic: Modern

Status: Active

Characteristic: Flashes twice every 10 seconds

Range: 18 miles

Position: 43° 03' 30 70° 41' 48

Note: Keeper Arnold White served here for 34 years (1907–1941)

A scatter of ship-killing rocks and ledges obstruct the entrance to the Piscataqua River and the approaches to New Hampshire's Portsmouth Harbor. Prominent among these is Whaleback Ledge Light, located just off Kittery Point, Maine, across the river from Portsmouth. A lighthouse marked the ledge as early as 1820, but it was destroyed by a storm in 1830. A second Whaleback tower built the following year gave way in a gale during the late 1860s. The 50-foot granite tower that marks Whaleback Ledge today was completed in 1872. Its fourth-order Fresnel lens was replaced by a modern optic after the station was automated in 1963.

TO SEE THE LIGHT: From U.S. 1A in York Harbor, follow Route 103 south for about four miles. Turn left onto Gerrish Island Lane and follow it to Pochohantas Road and Fort Foster. The park at Fort Foster offers excellent views of the light. The Isle of Shoals Steamship Company runs cruises offering excellent views of Whaleback and other lighthouses in the area; call (603) 431–5500.

Argand lamp

A clean-burning oil lamp widely used in lighthouses during the late eighteenth and early nineteenth centuries. Designed by French inventor Ami Argand, they produced an intense flame and a very bright light.

Automated light

A lighthouse with no keeper. Following World War II, remote control systems, light-activated switches, and fog-sensing devices made automation an increasingly cost-effective and attractive option. By 1970, only about sixty U.S. lighthouses still had full-time keepers, and within two decades, all but one of those beacons had been automated.

Beacon

A light or radio signal intended to guide mariners or aviators.

Breakwater light

Often harbors are protected from high waves by a lengthy barrier of stone called a breakwater. Because they rise only a few feet above the surface, breakwaters are hard to see, especially at night, and may threaten vessels entering or exiting the harbor. Breakwater beacons are meant to make mariners aware of this hazard and safely navigate the harbor entrance. For obvious reasons, the light tower usually is placed near the end of the breakwater.

Caisson towers

During the late nineteenth century, the government began building offshore lighthouses on caissons. A caisson was a hollow shell made of heavy, rolled-iron plates. Bolted together on land, the caisson was hauled to the construction site, sunk into the seabed up to a depth of about 30 feet, and then filled with sand, gravel, rock, or concrete.

Cast-iron towers

Introduced as a building material during the 1840s, cast iron revolutionized lighthouse construction. Stronger than stone and relatively light, cast iron made it possible to fabricate the parts of a light tower in a far-off foundry and then ship them to the construction site for assembly.

Characteristic

The identifying feature of a lighthouse beacon. To help mariners tell one beacon from another, maritime officials gave each light a distinct color or pattern of flashes.

Clockwork mechanism

Early rotating lighthouse lenses were often driven by a set of gears, weights, and pulleys similar to those used in large clocks. Every few hours, the keeper had to "rewind" the machinery by pulling or cranking the weights to the top of the tower.

Coast Guard

Since 1939, lighthouses and other aids to navigation in the United States have been the responsibility of the U.S. Coast Guard. Previously, the nation's maritime lights were maintained by a separate government agency, the U.S. Lighthouse Service.

Elevation or height of the focal plane

Fresnel lenses and most modern optical systems channel light signals into a narrow band known as the focal plane. Since the curvature of the earth would render low-lying lights practically worthless for navigation, a coastal beacon must have an elevated focal plane. The height of the plane above the water's surface—usually from 40 to 200 feet—helps determine the range of the light.

Fixed signal

A lighthouse beacon that shines constantly during its regular hours of operation is said to display a "fixed" signal.

Flashing signal

A lighthouse beacon that turns on and off or grows much brighter at regular intervals is called a flashing signal.

Fog signal or foghorn

A distinct sound signal, usually a horn, trumpet, or siren, used to warn vessels away from prominent headlands or navigational obstacles during periods of low visibility.

Fresnel lenses

Invented in 1822 by Augustin Fresnel, a
noted French physicist, Fresnel lenses
concentrate light into a powerful beam that
can be seen over great distances. Usually,
they consist of individual hand-polished
glass prisms arrayed in a bronze frame.
Manufactured by a number of French or
British companies, these devices came in
as many as eleven different sizes or
"orders." A massive first-order lens may be
more than six feet in diameter and twelve
feet tall, while a diminutive sixth-order lens
is only about one foot wide and not much
larger than an ordinary gallon jug.

The first-order Fresnel
lens at Seguin Island
Light.

Gallery

A circular walkway with a railing around the lantern. Galleries
provided keepers convenient access to the outside of the lantern for
window cleaning, painting, and repair work.

Harbor light

A beacon intended to assist vessels moving in and out of a harbor.
Not meant to serve as major coastal markers, harbor lights often
consisted of little more than a lantern hung from a pole. However,
many were official light stations with a tower and residence for
the keeper.

Keeper

Before the era of automation, operating and maintaining a light
station was in the hands of a keeper, sometimes aided by one or
more assistants. During the eighteenth and nineteenth centuries,
keepers were appointed by the Treasury Department or the president
himself in return for military service or a political favor. Although the
work was hard and the pay minimal, these appointments were
coveted since they offered a steady income and free housing.

Keeper's residence or dwelling

The presence of a keeper's residence is what turned a light station into a light "house." Sometime keepers lived in the tower itself, but a typical lighthouse dwelling was a detached one-and-a half-story wood or stone structure built in a style similar to that of other working-class homes in the area.

Lamp and reflector

For several decades prior to the introduction of the highly efficient Fresnel lens, lighthouse beacons were intensified by means of lamp-and-reflector systems. These combined a bright-burning lamp and a polished mirror shaped in a manner intended to concentrate the light.

Lantern

The glass-enclosed space at the top of a light tower which houses the lens or optic to protect it from the weather.

Lewis, Winslow

A former New England sea captain, Winslow Lewis built dozens of U.S. lighthouses during the first half of the nineteenth century. Lewis' bids for these projects were often quite low and the quality of the towers he built notoriously low. Lewis introduced his own version of the Argand lamp and reflector system—many considered it vastly inferior to the original.

Light tower

A tall, often cylindrical structure used to elevate a navigational light so that mariners can see it from a distance. Modern light towers support a lantern, which houses a lamp, electric beacon, or some other lighting device. Some light towers are an integral part of the station residence, but most are detached.

Lighthouse

A term applied to a wide variety of buildings constructed for the purpose of guiding ships. Often it is used interchangeably with similar or derivative terms such as "light tower," "light station," or the more general term "light."

Lighthouse Board

Beginning in 1851 and for more than half a century afterwards, U.S. lighthouses were administered by a Lighthouse Board consisting of nine members. Usually Board members were noted engineers, scientists, or military men. Creation of the Board brought a fresh professional spirit and penchant for innovation to the Lighthouse Service. Perhaps the Board's most telling change was adoption of the advanced Fresnel lens as the standard U.S. lighthouse optic.

Lighthouse Service

A common term applied to the various organizations or agencies that built and maintained U.S. lighthouses from 1789 until 1939 when the Coast Guard was placed in charge.

Light station

A navigational facility with a light beacon is commonly referred to as a light station. Often the term is used interchangeably with "light-house," but a light station may or may not include a tower, quarters for a keeper, or a fog signal.

Modern optic

Refers to a broad array of lightweight, mostly weatherproof devices that produce the most modern navigational lights.

Occulting or eclipsing light

There are several ways to produce a beacon that appears to flash. One is to "occult" or block the light at regular intervals, often with a rotating opaque panel.

Private aid to navigation

A privately owned and maintained navigational light. Often, such lights are formerly deactivated beacons that have been reestablished for historic or aesthetic purposes.

Range lights

Displayed in pairs, range lights help mariners keep their vessels safely within the narrow navigable channels that crisscross estuaries or lead in and out of harbors. The rear-range light is higher and further from the water than its partner, the front-range light, which is often located at water's edge. When viewed from mid-channel, the lights appear in perfect vertical alignment. If the upper light tilts either to the right or the left, a helmsman must steer in the opposite direction to correct course.

Skeleton towers

Iron or steel skeleton light towers consist of four or more heavily braced metal legs topped by workrooms and/or a lantern. Relatively durable and inexpensive, they were built in considerable numbers during the latter half of the nineteenth century. Small steel skeleton towers often take over the task of guiding mariners when the Coast Guard retires historic light stations such as the one on Dice Head in Castine, Maine.

Sparkplug, teakettle, or coffeepot lights

Many open-water lighthouses in northern climates are built on round, concrete-filled caissons, which protect them from fast-flowing water and ice floes. Usually, the massive caissons are black while the cylindrical iron towers on top of them are painted white giving them the appearance of an automobile spark plug. However, some think they look more like teakettles or coffeepots.

Wickies

Before electric power made lighthouse work much cleaner and simpler, nearly all navigational beacons were produced by oil or kerosene lamps. Most of these lamps had wicks that required constant care and trimming. Consequently, keepers often referred to themselves somewhat humorously as "wickies."

ABOUT THE AUTHORS

Photographs by **Bruce Roberts** have appeared in numerous magazines, including *Life* and *Sports Illustrated*, and in hundreds of books, many of them about lighthouses. He was director of photography at *Southern Living* magazine for many years. His work is also on display in the permanent collection at the Smithsonian Institution. He lives in Morehead City, North Carolina.

Ray Jones is the author or coauthor of fourteen best-selling books about lighthouses. He has served as an editor at Time-Life Books, as founding editor of *Albuquerque Living* magazine, as writing coach at *Southern Living* magazine, and as founding publisher of Country Roads Press. He lives in Pebble Beach, California, where he continues to write about lighthouses and serves as a consultant to businesses, publishers, and other authors.

ALSO BY BRUCE ROBERTS AND RAY JONES

Lighthouses of California
A Guidebook and Keepsake

Lighthouses of Florida
A Guidebook and Keepsake

Lighthouses of Massachusetts
A Guidebook and Keepsake

New England Lighthouses
Maine to Long Island Sound

American Lighthouses
A Comprehensive Guide

Eastern Great Lakes Lighthouses
Ontario, Erie, and Huron

Western Great Lakes Lighthouses
Michigan and Superior

Gulf Coast Lighthouses
Florida Keys to the Rio Grande

Mid-Atlantic Lighthouses
Hudson River to Chesapeake Bay

Pacific Northwest Lighthouses
Oregon, Washington, Alaska, and British Columbia

Southern Lighthouses
Outer Banks to Cape Florida